# *Professional Supervision*

## Myths, Culture and Structure

*Eileen O Neill*
*2004*

Published by

RMA PUBLICATIONS
St Bernard's, Rocklow Rd, Fethard, Co Tipperary, IRELAND

Copyright © Eileen O'Neill, 2004

All rights reserved. No part of this publication may be reproduced, stored in a retrieval system or transmitted inany form or by any means, without written permission from the publisher.

Published by

RMA PUBLICATIONS
St Bernard's, Rocklow Rd,
Fethard, Co Tipperary, IRELAND
www.rma.ie

ISBN 0-9548432-0-7

Published 2004

*Designed & Printed by the Limerick Leader*

## About the Author
Professional experience spanning thirty years, which includes working with staff and management, at all stages of their practice development, coupled with a Higher Diploma and an M.A. in Child Care and Protection Studies is some of what Eileen O'Neill brings to her work.
She is strongly influenced by her work in community based services and particularly in residential child care where she spent time as a practitioner before becoming involved in the development and provision of Professional Supervision, Training and Staff Development. She has been actively involved at national level on a number of working parties to promote best practice and has contributed to third level course development.
She provides independent training, consultancy and team development programmes to meet identified needs of organisations, in social care and in the wider health care sector with a range of disciplines.
He work in Professional Supervision reflects a strong commitment to ensuring quality service delivery through improved standards and practice. She has published articles and addressed conferences on the subject and is currently working on a practice-based model for the evaluation of Professional Supervision. This is her first book.
E-mail: oneilleileen@ireland.com

## About the RMA
The RMA has been the Professional and Representative Organization of Directors and Managers in Residential Child and Youth Care since 1932. The RMA is committed to:
Advancing the education and training of Managers and Child Care Workers.
Informing Government Departments and other relevant bodies on issues of child care and actively participating with them in the foundation of child care policy and reform of child and family law.
Encouraging the development of an integrated Child Care service by promoting co-operation and understanding between the different agencies concerned with the welfare of children.
Promoting research into residential care and other areas of child care in order to influence policy and practice.
Representing the views of the Resident Managers when necessary on matters of child care policy and practice.
E-mail info@rma.ie   Web: www.rma.ie

# Contents

Acknowledgements

Introduction . . . . . . . . . . . . . . . . . . . . . . . . . . . . . . . . . . . . . . . i

## Part One

Why? Professional Supervision as part of the wider picture . . . . 3
What is Professional Supervision? . . . . . . . . . . . . . . . . . . . . . . 13
Functions of Professional Supervision . . . . . . . . . . . . . . . . . . . 21
Dual Focus Approach . . . . . . . . . . . . . . . . . . . . . . . . . . . . . . . 29
Induction, Appraisal and the links to Supervision . . . . . . . . . . . 35
Who Needs Supervision? . . . . . . . . . . . . . . . . . . . . . . . . . . . . . 41
Myths . . . . . . . . . . . . . . . . . . . . . . . . . . . . . . . . . . . . . . . . . . . 45

## Part Two

Providing Effective Supervision . . . . . . . . . . . . . . . . . . . . . . . . 55
Supervision Policy and Procedures . . . . . . . . . . . . . . . . . . . . . 61
Skills and Tasks of the Supervisor . . . . . . . . . . . . . . . . . . . . . . 77
Supervising the Student . . . . . . . . . . . . . . . . . . . . . . . . . . . . . . 93
Case Studies . . . . . . . . . . . . . . . . . . . . . . . . . . . . . . . . . . . . . . 99
Beginnings and Endings . . . . . . . . . . . . . . . . . . . . . . . . . . . . . 105
*What If?* . . . . . . . . . . . . . . . . . . . . . . . . . . . . . . . . . . . . . . . . . 111

Appendix . . . . . . . . . . . . . . . . . . . . . . . . . . . . . . . . . . . . . . . . 117
Reference and Bibliography . . . . . . . . . . . . . . . . . . . . . . . . . . 123

# Acknowledgements

This book owes its existence to many people who have, knowingly and at times unknowingly, contributed to my ongoing interest and involvement in the development of the practice and process of Professional Supervision over the last twenty years. To all of these I wish to express my gratitude, with a special word of thanks to the following:

- To all of you who entered into supervisory partnerships with me over a lifetime of work and from whom I continue to learn. Thank you for taking risks in sharing so much and in the process, challenging me to further develop my understanding and skills.
- To many practitioners and managers in numerous organisations and disciplines throughout the country. Your constant requests, for an Irish text on Professional Supervision, which would provide guidance and provoke debate, acted as a catalyst for this book. Your belief in my capacity to undertake the task acted as a spur to attempt it. Thank you.
- Special thanks to the Resident Managers Association, sponsor and publisher - your trust that the finished product would be worthy of publication was refreshing. Your support and patience have been reassuring and ensured that I kept writing.
- To John Deeley for your meticulous attention to detail as proof-reader and to Eoin Moriarity, of the Limerick Leader, who designed the cover and was responsible for the printing. Thank you both for bringing your expertise and support to this undertaking.
- To Samantha Ronan for your insightful comments in discussions and to Monica McElvaney and Triona Dunne for your ready willingness in reading the final draft, at short notice. Your comments provided clarity and added greatly to the finished work - thank you.
- Many thanks to Patrica Kennifick for the numerous discussions and sharing of ideas over the years, it proves enjoyable as well as productive.

- To Noeleen Price who provided constructive feedback and invaluable suggestions at various stages of the writing of this book. Sincere thanks for your constant support, objectivity and humour which kept me going at times of confusion and doubt.

- To my family and especially Fergus, whose love, understanding and acceptance make it all worthwhile.

I acknowledge and accept responsibility for any mistakes that may appear - they are mine and mine alone.

# Introduction

This text is tangible evidence of "reflective practice". It draws on experiences, over many years, of involvement in all aspects of the practice and process of Professional Supervision.

My practice and thinking regarding Supervision continue to be expanded and challenged by a significant range of experiences. Among these are:

- Direct work in Supervision, with individuals and with staff teams, which has acted as a catalyst for much of what lies in these pages.
- Developing and implementing models and structures for Supervision at organisational level, across disciplines, in both the voluntary and statutory sectors, has further contributed to my understanding of the issues surrounding Supervision.
- Designing, delivering and evaluating specific training programmes on Professional Supervision, for practitioners at all stages of their professional development in a wide range of services, ensures that I keep up to date and challenged regarding all aspects of what I practice and believe.
- My own Supervision which, through questioning and reflection, provides me with the place and space to continually grow and to develop my insights, while ensuring my practice remains at all times accountable and focused on the needs of those who use the Services.

I am influenced by all of these factors and by my experience of the significant role that realistic Professional Supervision can play in the delivery of quality care and effective service delivery across a growing range of disciplines. Among the disciplines referred to are: Child Care, Social Work, Nursing, Occupational Therapy, Social Care, Speech and Language Therapy, Play Therapy, Psychology, Physiotherapy, Youth Work and Community Development.

The impetus for this text is threefold.

Firstly, it comes at a time in Ireland when much attention is being paid to the nature of care being delivered to people at times of vulnerability or need in their lives. The combination of public disquiet at the level of emerging scandals and abuse in our society and services, the growing body of legislation relating to accountability and the ongoing public expectation for higher standards and measurable outcomes all highlight the need for a recognised framework for accountable practice and for the ongoing development of staff in a supportive environment.

Secondly, the increased attention to the provision of Supervision which is relevant, accessible and effective has highlighted a demand for guidelines for its realistic implementation. This is particularly evident in the ad hoc and at times reactive manner in which Supervision has developed in a range of services, often more influenced by individual interpretation (usually by the supervisor) than by informed understanding of Supervision.

Thirdly, numerous requests from practitioners, managers and more recently, administrators, for an expansion of an earlier and brief text on Professional Supervision (2000), acted as a catalyst for this text.

This book is written for anyone with an interest in Supervision. This includes those with indirect involvement in the supervisory process as well as those who participate directly in Supervision. It is intended as an introduction to Professional Supervision for those who are coming to it for the first time and to act as a trigger to further debate among those who are familiar with it through their practice and experience. To ensure that Supervision is used as a realistic and effective resource, its functions and process need to be fully understood and valued by practitioners, managers, administrators and funding agents alike.

Put simply, this book could be described as exploring the *Why, What* and *How* of Professional Supervision. In so exploring, it does not purport to provide definitive answers to the questions but rather to present some signposts towards answers which may, in fact, raise even more questions in the process. Definitive answers in relation to Supervision suggest there is only one way to go - that has not been my experience to date. However, clear guidelines and principles need to underpin all of what we do.

Divided into two parts, the text poses three general questions.

Part 1
- The question **Why** Supervision? is explored. This examines some of the factors which contribute to the need for formal Supervision across a range of disciplines.
- **What** is Supervision? is then considered and a number of the components which contribute to its effectiveness are highlighted.
- Induction, Supervision and Performance Reviews and the links between each are outlined.
- The main functions of Supervision are discussed and the reader is introduced to a *Dual Focus Approach* to Supervision, which has a cross discipline application.
- Attention is focused on who needs Supervision and Part 1 concludes with an exploration (and hopefully an explosion) of some common myths which surround Supervision.

Part 2
- The second part examines a significant number of issues pertaining to the frequently posed question **How** *does effective Supervision take place?* It outlines some practical considerations for the introduction and implementation of professional Supervision at organisational and individual levels.
- The components necessary for the development and implementation of effective Supervision Policy and Procedures are outlined and discussed. The influence of the organisational culture on the effectiveness, or otherwise, of Supervision is considered.

- Specific tasks and skills of the supervisor are identified and explored.
- Guidelines are provided for both a first Supervision meeting and a final Supervision meeting between the supervisor and supervisee. Supervising the student is also discussed with guidelines for regular supervisory meetings.
- Case studies provide the reader with an introduction to participants in the supervisory process.
- Some frequently asked questions regarding Supervision are identified with comment.

The appendices contain a sample of forms frequently used in connection with Supervision. These include a Supervision Contract, Recording Sheet and Transfer Form.

Two sections of an earlier piece of my work, a version of *Myths* (page 45) and the case study entitled *Lillian* (page 99) which appeared in the European Journal of Social Education in 2003 were based on a workshop I presented to the FESET Conference in Italy in November 2002.These have been expanded for inclusion here.

Professional Supervision, as described, encompasses not only the principles of Clinical Supervision but also the wider context of the individual in their practice. The terms *Professional Supervision* and *Supervision* are used interchangeably throughout.

# *Professional Supervision*

## *Myths, Culture and Structure*

*Part 1*

# *Why? Professional Supervision as part of the wider picture*

Professional Supervision has been recognised as a valuable and necessary component of practice among some disciplines, it has also been a frequently misunderstood and often underused resource for others.

Structured Supervision is generally accepted as part of practice in some disciplines - these include Social Work and Residential Child Care services as well as Psychology and Social Care. The introduction of structured Supervision is a relatively new undertaking in other disciplines. Nursing, Youth and Community Development Work, Speech and Language Therapy are examples of some of these.

A number of factors influence the current attention being paid to the importance of Supervision and its development or introduction across a range of disciplines. To set Supervision in context this section considers some of the factors that underpin the need for effective Professional Supervision practice and policies.

## Professional Requirements

Direct references are made to the Supervision requirements for practitioners in specific disciplines by national standards and professional bodies as is evident in the following examples.

## Residential Child Care
National Standards for Children's Residential Centres (2001)
Standard 2 - Management and Staffing
2.13 and 2.14 *"All staff members receive regular and formal supervision, the details of which are recorded. There is an effective link between supervision and the implementation of individual placement plans."*


## Nursing
The Final Report of the Review of the Scope of Practice for Nursing and Midwifery (2000)
The importance of accountability for practice, support for the individual and the need for continued professional development in the sector are all highlighted in the report. The Report considers the importance of Supervision for nurses and midwives and states that *"Consideration of the types of Supervision necessary for midwives in both hospitals and community settings is needed"* (4.5.5)


## Occupational Therapy
Code of Ethics and Professional Conduct for Occupational Therapists
5.2 Supervision, Support and Review
5.2.1 *"A Member has a responsibility to seek support and formal supervision and to ensure that these needs are communicated to employing organisations."*
5.2.2 *"The member's level of professional knowledge and expertise should be continually reviewed by self assessment and by regular updating in the interests of high quality care."*


## Social Work
Recommendations of the Council of Europe
The Recommendations of the Committee of Ministers to member states on Social Workers adopted on the 17th January (2001) states that *"initial*

*education and training must be part of an ongoing process including life-long learning and opportunities for advanced education"* Rec. (2001)1. Supervision is long recognised as a core component in the practice of Social Work.

## *Psychology*

The Psychological Society of Ireland
*Guidelines for Registered Membership* (2000) make specific reference to the need for graduate members who wish to become registered members needing to clarify *"how training or work experience can be supervised and subsequently attested to..."* and outline the detail requirements regarding time and frequency.
Further references are made to supervision in the Articles of Association and Code of Professional Ethics 9.
The Professional Practice Guidelines (1995) of the British Psychological Society identify the importance of post qualification Supervision. *"In order to maintain the quality of performance and to extend a psychologists range of skills, Supervision should be organised for all levels and grades of experience".*

Coupled with the requirements of the specific disciplines, references are also made to the need for structured Supervision in a significant number of Inquiry Reports in the last 20 years.

## **Inquiry findings**

Unfortunately, the past two decades have shown that not all practice was as positive or indeed as safe as expected for those who used the services. Evidence now exists of:
- Poor communication between professionals (Kilkenny Incest Investigation Report 1993).
- Services being expected to be all things to all people (Madonna House Report 1996)

- Fragmentation in service provision and unclear lines of accountability (West of Ireland Farmer Case 1998)

Such reports highlighted the absence of regular, structured Supervision and one of the common factors running through the recommendations of these and numerous other reports is the need for such a framework, particularly for those employed in areas offering care and protection to others. This is further borne out by the findings of Inquiry Reports in the U.K. such as the Cleveland Report (1987), the Tyra Hendley Inquiry (1987) and the Pindown Report (1989).

In recommending that Supervision be provided for staff working in child protection, the Kilkenny Incest Investigation Report (1993) identified the components of effective Supervision as follows:

"Supervision facilitates learning, provides an opportunity to plan and evaluate work and supports workers. Supervision also promotes good standards of practice to the benefit of the public."

In 2003, the Victoria Climbié Inquiry Report stressed the importance of the responsibility and accountability of everyone at every level in the organisation for the protection and well-being of vulnerable children and their families. In its Summary and Recommendations the report stated that "Directors of Social Services must ensure that the work of staff working directly with children is regularly supervised." (Laming 2003, Recommendation 45)

It is incumbent on both practitioners and employers, who have significant responsibility for the delivery of safe effective care to people at times of need, to ensure tangible learning from the omissions and mistakes of the past. Providing and actively participating in Professional Supervision is one way of redressing the gaps and mistakes of the past to ensure quality service to those who need it.

## Government Publications

A number of recent government publications are influential in contributing to the current awareness, among professionals and administrators alike, of the need to provide structured arrangements for the ongoing management, training and support of staff in the health sector. A number of these reports make explicit and implicit reference to Supervision in this regard.

- ***The Children First National Guidelines for the Protection and Welfare of Children (1999)***
Writing in the Foreword to these Guidelines, the then Minister of State with Responsibility for Children described Children First as providing *"professionals with a set of sound principles and good practice guidelines"*. These Guidelines recognise the importance of the role of Supervision for staff in child protection work and in managing the associated stresses involved. It states:
    > *"It is essential that managers of all disciplines involved in child protection acknowledge the levels of actual or potential stress that may affect their staff and take steps to address the problem. These steps include ... adequate and regular supervision of staff".*

- ***The National Children's Strategy - Our Children - Their Lives(2000)***
This document is seen as *"a tool to be used in developing the partnerships necessary to deliver action to enhance the status and improve the quality of life for Ireland's children."*
In identifying the action proposed to facilitate working with *"children with additional needs"*, the Strategy states that *"staff will be supported and developed to ensure that they have the necessary level of knowledge and expertise and have available to them skilled supervision and support."*
National Children's Strategy (2000)

- ***National Health Strategy (2001)***
Arising from the National Health Strategy *"Quality and Fairness - A Health System for You"* (2001) the *"Action Plan for People Management in the*

*Health Service"* was launched in 2002. Up to 93,000 full-time employees in the Health Service (at the end of 2001) play a vital role in the delivery of service in a variety of settings to the public. It stands to reason therefore that ensuring effective service delivery through its employees requires a clearly identified overall plan which is delivered with agreed structures at local level. This Action Plan identified both operational and strategic issues to *"address very real and tangible issues",* and while acknowledging that *"people management is only one aspect in the broader Human Resource Management agenda",* it nonetheless recognised that *"it is an essential element that must be improved"* (2002).

Seven themes were identified to progress the Action Plan as follows:
- o Managing People Effectively
- o Improving the Quality of Working Life
- o Devising and Implementing Best Practice
- o Employment Policies and Procedures
- o Developing the Partnership Approach
- o Investing in Training, Development and Education
- o Promoting Improved Employee and Industrial Relations
- o Developing Performance Management

There is a clear link between the core functions of effective Supervision and the main thrust of the principles outlined in the themes of the Action Plan for People Management. Ensuring accountability for practice, as well as facilitating ongoing and relevant learning and development for employees in a supportive working environment, are the core functions of all Professional Supervision. The objectives of the action plan for people management as outlined can be met through implementing structured Supervision in an organisation. This recognises, in a tangible way, staff as the major resource in any sector and provides a partnership forum to improve practice, management and service delivery.

The Office for Health Management have outlined a working strategy for the implementation of Personal Development Planning (PDP) and recognise it as a *"continuous development process that enables people to make the best use of their skills and helps advance both the individual's plans and the strategy goals of the organisation"* ( Personal Development Planning, 2003). Participation in Personal Development Planning is voluntary and is carried out with one's line manager. It facilitates planning for ongoing development and it usually occurs at fixed points in the career of the individual. Supervision is an ongoing, continuous process, as opposed to a series of fixed events. It provides the contextual setting for Personal Development Planning to take place regularly throughout the individual's career with a designated supervisor who may or may not be the line manager. Usually, Supervision is a professional, discipline or organisational requirement and is not voluntary.

Investing in training, development and education is a laudable task and needs to be connected to improved daily practice to prove a worthwhile investment for all involved in delivering and receiving services. Ensuring that training is integrated effectively into ongoing practice requires more than just the opportunity to attend or participate in the training event. It is enhanced when the participant is expected to reflect on the learning gained and to demonstrate clear links to daily practice. This can be facilitated through regular individual and group Supervision.

Professional Supervision which facilitates organisational learning as well as individual learning will ensure that services continue to grow and develop in a proactive way while drawing on the strengths of all employees and not just based on the views of the few, hence ensuring a partnership approach.

## Duty of Care

The employer's duty of care is another factor in the current introduction and on-going development of Supervision policies and practices in many areas.

Eardly (2002) writing on Bullying and Stress in the Workplace explains a duty of care as *"when one person owes another because of the nature of the relationship between them"*. He further states *"The relationship* between employer and employee is one in which a duty of care is owed." This common law rule has been *"incorporated and supplanted by legislation"* in the 1989 Safety, Health and Welfare at Work Act, thereby placing explicit duty of care on employers for employees.

Reference is made to duty of care, particularly to those working in the area of child protection, in a legal opinion provided to the Insurer and Risk Management Advisors to the Health Boards, Irish Public Mutual Bodies, in relation to reducing the risk of litigation in child protection practices (Power 1997).

Tangible evidence of a response to such *duty of care* is evident in many large organisations in the public and private sectors. This is particularly so in regard to employers providing supportive mechanisms for staff. Many services now have, among their staff, personnel trained in Critical Incident Stress Debriefing to support staff in the aftermath of serious crises or incidents. Employee Assistance Programmes, which are available through Employee Assistance Officers, in Health Boards and other organisations that employ large numbers, act as an independent form of support for those employed.

Professional Supervision which focuses on the Work with direct connection to the Person doing the work is tangible evidence of the employers' response to their duty of care to employees. As well as providing a supportive forum, effective Supervision also facilitates the ongoing development of the individual in the context of accountable work practices.

## Staff retention

It is widely acknowledged that staff are the principal and pivotal resource in all areas of health care. More than 80% of the budget in any Health Board goes on staff salaries and it can cost an average of one million euro to employ a professional throughout their working life. It follows therefore that effective recruitment processes and ongoing initiatives to retain staff are

vital to protect and nurture this investment on behalf of the public.
Staff are less likely to leave a job where they feel satisfied, worthwhile and respected. At a time of recognised staff shortages in the public services, particularly the health sector, it is worth considering a link between effective Supervision and staff retention.

A number of staff are leaving their chosen work due increasingly to stress and stress - related conditions. This is evident in research undertaken on Social Workers leaving posts in this country (Fulham 1997) where unmanageable caseloads, feelings of worthlessness as well as stress were cited as some of the contributing factors.

Research carried out by Sinclair and Gibbs (1998) found that *"regular formal supervision is important for staff morale".*

The Review of the Scope of Practice for Nursing and Midwifery (2000) when considering Supervision said that *"...the evidence that exists suggests that it (Supervision) is a useful means of improving job satisfaction of staff and provides them with a means of reflection on practice which can benefit patient care."* (4.5.3)

Evidence exists of staff feeling more motivated and confident to carry out their responsibilities when participating in regular effective Professional Supervision as part of their practice.

Supervision, as part of an overall framework for professional practice development, recognises, in a tangible way, staff as the major resource. It allows them time and space to re-focus on their overall task in an accountable and supportive context. It facilitates the identification of areas of their practice which need further development and can thus re-charge their batteries.

In summary, the following can be identified as contributory factors to why Professional Supervision is deemed necessary:

- Professional Task - the professional dimension to a discipline requires recognition, structure and monitoring.
- Accountability - Practitioners must be accountable and held accountable for **what** they do and for **how** they do it. Employers need to have structures in place which facilitate this process.
- Inquiry Reports - Inquiries, into service deficits and abuse in the past, identify the absence of regular, formal Supervision for a range of staff in the health sector. The recommendations of these reports strongly advocate its responsible availability and use. Evidence of learning from the gaps and mistakes of the past must be seen to be integrated into responsible practice.
- Workers are recognised as a vital resource - Investment in the human resources of services can aid staff retention and is recognised as beneficial for effective and improved delivery of services.
- Continued Professional Development is perceived now more than ever as a necessary component for practitioners at all stages of their career.
- Duty of Care and recognition of demanding work - The employer must provide supports and structures to enable staff to work in demanding and potentially stressful working environments.

# *What is Professional Supervision?*

## Confusion regarding Professional Supervision

Confusion often exists regarding what exactly Supervision is and how it needs to be carried out. To understand this, it is necessary to recognise that for many disciplines Supervision has been either parachuted in as a response to a particular crisis or concern or else it has been transplanted directly from one discipline to another with little if any thought regarding its specific purpose and function in the newly placed discipline. This is unfair on practitioners and unfair on Supervision.

The lack of structured training and development for those with supervisory responsibility has further contributed to an ad hoc development of Supervision practice. Supervisors have frequently had to rely on their own experiences as supervisees to inform their subsequent role as supervisor. This often leads on the one hand to the supervisor attempting to recreate the positive experiences of Supervision s/he may have received, or on the other hand, being determined to avoid the more negative aspects of their own Supervision for their supervisee. Unfortunately, neither of these approaches guarantees effective Supervision.

Even where Supervision is an established part of professional practice (Social Work, Residential Child Care), the experience of many practitioners is that, in the absence of recognised policy and procedures, the Supervision they receive is strongly dependent on the interpretation of their individual supervisor rather than on a recognised and agreed understanding of its purpose and function.

Books have been written which have explored Supervision. A significant number of practitioners have been actively and effectively engaged in Supervision during their working life ... yet confusion still exists among many as to exactly what Professional Supervision is. Unfortunately for many people the very term *Supervision* conjures up images of someone standing over their shoulder checking up on them or watching over what they do. Replacing this image with one that views it as *Super-Vision* is necessary to ensure that the resource of Supervision is used effectively to facilitate greater and improved vision regarding practice.

Due to the differing experiences of Supervision which exist, it may be useful to identify some of the things that *do not* constitute Supervision before considering what Supervision is.

## Supervision is not...

- A casual activity that takes place over a cup of coffee
- A chat
- Counselling
- An optional extra
- Something you only do when there is a problem
- Appraisal
- Support for the supervisor
- A telling-off
- A grievance session
- A test or exam
- Something you only do when there's nothing else happening

If Supervision is seen within the organisation as a casual activity or simply as a chat with another then it is not being provided or used effectively as a valuable resource. If this happens then the content is likely to drift with no clear focus and little if any positive outcome in the long term for either participants or service. This casual experience of Supervision has contributed to the confusion felt by some regarding its purpose and value and to the resistance or half - hearted commitments experienced by others who may have expected more from it.

The structured format of Supervision contributes to its purpose and functions being recognised and respected. This allows it to meet its objectives which are to ensure quality, relevant care and service to those who use the services in the most effective and efficient way.

Supervision and counselling are two distinct resources and should not be confused. Counselling skills are used in a significant amount of work involving interpersonal communication and engagement. The Supervisor, in the course of supervising, uses a range of skills which include counselling skills - so does the nurse in interacting with a patient, and the social worker in establishing contact with a family and the speech and language therapist in engaging with the client. They all draw on counselling skills in order to enable them to carry out specific aspects of their role; it does not mean that they are there as a counsellor to the patient or client.

Some of the confusion which exists between counselling and Supervision could be linked to past practices. These included, for some disciplines, sourcing Supervision externally from counsellors, psychologists or psychotherapists, as they were the main practitioners where Supervision was an integral part of their training and practice. This may have contributed to how these two processes and practices, Supervision and counselling, began to become connected for some - regardless of the actual experience of Supervision which they received.

The difference between counselling and Supervision needs to be clearly understood by the supervisee, the organisation and especially by the supervisor. Very simply, counselling is for the benefit of the person as an individual, whereas Supervision is for the benefit of the person as a practitioner to enable them to carry out their professional responsibilities. The former may contribute to the latter but this is a by-product of the process and not its main objective.

Development of specific models, structures and processes for Supervision within a range of disciplines (which meet their specific needs) is contributing to greater clarity regarding the differences between Supervision and counselling.

Frequently and unfortunately for some, Supervision has been equated only with problems in some services. "Problem only" Supervision suggests a reactive culture and climate in any organisation and limits the effective development, not only of the individual worker but also of the service itself. If the scope of Supervision is limited to being focused only on problems then Supervision can not and is not meeting its objectives. In turn, it becomes connected solely with difficulties and thereby can develop a negative association. It is not unusual in these circumstances for Supervision to be avoided, or for the supervisee to be anxious, apprehensive or even resentful. Resentment is understandable if the only direct or formal contact with the supervisor in to discuss difficulties or problems. It is of course important that Supervision is available in response to a problem, concern or difficulty but this should be in addition to the regular Supervision which has many uses. It may be worth considering whether "Problem only" Supervision warrants being called Supervision at all?

Supervision cannot be seen or used as a grievance session by either participant. There may be times when the supervisee needs the safety of Supervision to say what they are really feeling about an event or a colleague but it is the responsibility of the supervisor to ensure that the focus remains on the individual supervisee and on the task at hand.

At times students undertaking Placements as part of their college courses equate Supervision with being an exam or test of their performance. Such a view of Supervision during Placement raises questions about the overall Placement experience available to the student and about the student's preparation for Placement in the first instance. In any well-structured and planned Placement, Supervision forms only one component. Unfortunately and all too often in some disciplines, Supervision has been the only structured aspect of the placement; the rest of the time the student can feel left to their own devices with little direction or guidance between Supervision meetings. This is not conducive to the effective development of the emerging professional practitioner. Their Supervision then takes on the only formal aspect of contact with the supervisor and is understandably seen by them as a "test" of their performance. The student then has limited opportunity to develop his/her understanding and use of Supervision as a professional resource. In such circumstances the student frequently leaves the Placement with a narrow view of the value and role of Supervision within the workplace. This, for many, can contribute to anxiety in the future when presented with regular, formal Supervision as an expected part of their work as qualified practitioners.

If Supervision is something that only happens when there is nothing else happening then, in many organisations, it will never happen. The overall workloads of practitioners are so full that Supervision will never happen unless it is prioritised by the service in a culture which recognises and values the significant contribution that it makes to improved professional practice.

## Professional Supervision is…

Supervision has been defined in a number of ways. These have included definitions from the fields of counselling, social work and more recently nursing. It has variously been described as a process, developed in response to perceived needs, which allows for the supportive learning of the individual while ensuring accountability for practice.

Professional Supervision is a partnership process between the supervisor, the supervisee and the organisation and as such provides a regular, structured opportunity to discuss work, to reflect on practice and progress and to plan for future development. The reality of Supervision is that it involves at least two parties, the supervisor and the supervisee, both of whom have distinct responsibilities within this process. These shared responsibilities are evident in defining Supervision as a partnership.

The core process of Supervision takes place in regular, planned, structured time which ensures the standard of care to those who use the services and facilitates the workers professional development and support. In addition to regular planned meetings, circumstances may also require the provision of Supervision at other times, for example in response to a difficulty, concern or crisis.

Regular structured Supervision provides an opportunity to:
- Reflect on the content and process of practice
- Monitor and ensure the quality of work.
- Review and plan work.
- Consider any particular responsibilities and input of the supervisee.
- Develop understanding and skills.
- Seek and receive information, support and feedback.
- Voice and examine concerns.
- Explore and express issues brought up by the work.
- Consider the impact of the work on the supervisee.
- Be proactive.
- Be challenged constructively.
- Identify skills and strengths of the worker.
- Identify areas requiring further development.
- Agree targets for future development in the context of a Professional Development Plan (PDP) and identify training needs.
- Monitor and evaluate ongoing development and aspects of the Professional Development Plan.

Seen in this way Supervision is a positive resource, which benefits all those involved in ensuring safe, effective care and service delivery. However, all too often Supervision has been used solely as a response to either a crisis or a problem. This is not an effective use of Professional Supervision and can add to the avoidance and resistance at times experienced by some in the supervisory partnership. Supervision must be available at times of difficulties and crises but must also be provided on a regular basis.

Supervision can take place on a one to one basis or in a group or team context - whatever the context; the principles and functions are clearly the same.

Overall, Supervision can be viewed as a response to needs
- *"the need of the worker to be supported, challenged and developed in a demanding, complex and often stressful working environment;*
- *the need of the service user (client) for safe quality care at times of need;*
- *the need of the organisation to ensure best practice and accountability of its employees." (O Neill 2000)*

Professional Supervision is the partnership process of ongoing reflection and feedback between a named supervisor and supervisee/s to ensure and enhance effective practice.

# *Functions of Professional Supervision*

Accountability, Support and Learning are the main functions of Professional Supervision.

Accountability in Supervision is for safe, effective practice. Support is for workers to carry out their responsibilities in demanding and potentially stressful working environments. Learning is for the ongoing learning and continued development and self awareness of the individual employees and of the service.

Professional Supervision provides a structured channel for the functions of accountability, support and learning to be met. It is the interrelationship, over time, between these three functions that leads to effective Supervision. One function will not work successfully without being considered in the context of the other two.

Kadushin (1976) and Proctor (1986) have identified the functions similarly using the following terms: the managerial or normative function, the supportive or restorative function and the educative or formative function.

Richards and Payne (1990) and Morrison (1995) include mediation as a fourth function of Supervision. However, it could also be viewed that if the other three functions are successfully incorporated into the process and practice of Supervision then mediation is automatically subsumed throughout and not a separate or distinct function. The main functions of accountability, support and learning are those considered here, while acknowledging that mediation could also be a specific function within some disciplines or organisations.

To ensure that Supervision meets its objectives each of these three functions need to be included in a balanced way over time. Otherwise there is a risk of Supervision becoming focused on one aspect with the likelihood of 'Check-list Supervision' taking place, (Hawkins & Shohet 1994). However, it must be stressed that the supervisor who over emphasises this balance risks using these functions as a checklist in themselves. This would prevent the interaction and engagement between themselves and the supervisee emerging. This dynamic contributes to the process, which in and of itself can facilitate effective Supervision.

*Figure 1*

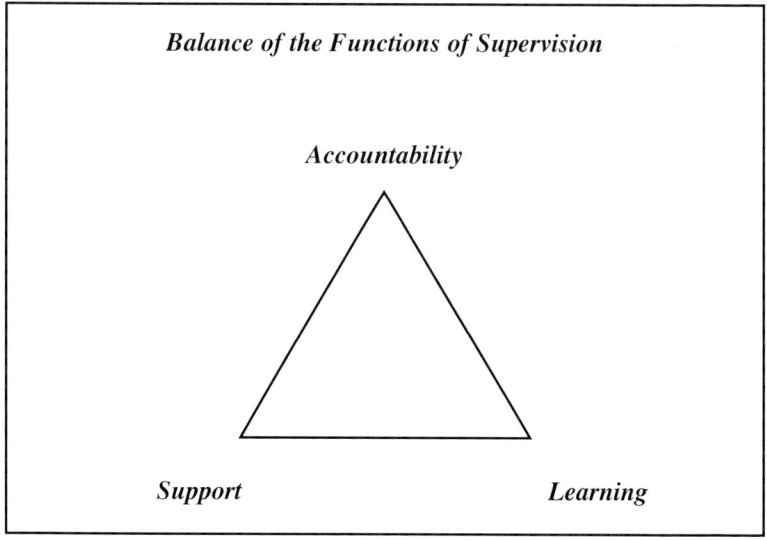

**(Based on Kadushin 1976)**

## Accountability

The word Accountability consists of two words Account and Ability and is defined in the dictionary as *"liability and/or responsibility"* and *"able to be explained"*. Being accountable is said to be *"responsible to someone or for some action"* while words that are used interchangeably include *"answerable, liable, and obligated"* (Collins 1989).
Accountability has also been described as *"the fulfilment of a formal obligation to disclose to referent others the purposes, principles, procedures, relationships, results, income and expenditures for which one has authority"*. (Lewis and Batey,1982).

From the time an employment contract is signed all employees of any organisation or service are accountable for their practice. Accountability is **not just for what** is done but **also for how** the job is carried out. The practitioner must be able to identify and justify the reasons for decisions made *"in the context of legislation, professional standards, evidence based practice and professional and ethical conduct."* (An Bord Altranais 2000).

The perception that qualification is an end in itself is no longer accepted in today's climate. This has been significantly challenged by the commitment to continued professional development evident among many professional bodies and echoed in the National Health Strategy; Quality and Fairness; A Health System for You (2001) and the subsequent *"Action Plan for People Management in the Health Service"* (2002).

Employers have a responsibility to ensure that those they employ are accountable and held accountable for what they do and for how they do it.

The ultimate accountability is to the people who use the services. They are entitled to the highest standards of care and service possible and it is to them that all practitioners are fundamentally accountable.

Evidence from the past highlights that it was often taken for granted that those working in responsible positions were, by definition, carrying out their work in a responsible manner. Sadly, as evidenced in media reports and court cases of recent times, this is not always the case.

The need for greater accountability is recognised in all areas of society, in business and political arenas as well as in the caring professions. It is not always enough to assume, just because a policy or guideline exists relating to a specific area of practice, that it is being carried out accordingly or that it is understood. It is important that some structure is in place to monitor and ensure safe, quality practice - this is one of the functions of management.

Working with people, at times of vulnerability or need in their lives, demands practitioners of the highest calibre. Such practitioners must be clearly accountable and held accountable for all aspects of their practice. Ensuring that all those employed in the care and protection of others have structured opportunities for Professional Supervision - to review their practice, receive regular feedback, plan their work and identify their ongoing development - is one way in which employers facilitate accountable practice.

## Support

*Why is support considered necessary for practitioners? Surely if they are trained they should be competent to do the job without needing support.* This is not an unheard of comment from some people.

Support in the context of Professional Supervision does not mean support of the *"there, there, you'll be all right"* variety, nor is it the type of support which has the potential to become a crutch, in other words, repetitive support in order to help the person from one crisis to another. This type of support is ineffective and has no place in professional practice let alone in Professional Supervision.

Effective Support in Supervision is about a range of factors:
- It is about honest feedback from which tangible learning and self awareness can and does take place.
- It is about providing a supportive environment where mistakes are acknowledged and owned in order to facilitate improved practice.
- It is about the opportunity to reflect on what has taken place (the good as well as that which requires improvement) in order to do it even better the next time.
- It is about affirmation for work done and for the effort required to do it - in difficult and at times thankless conditions.
- It is about having a place where the stresses and demands of the work can be openly explored and reflected on, so that they do not become a block to the work or a further pressure which could lead to possible sickness or burnout.

Being challenged in a respectful manner is sometimes the most supportive thing that can be done for another. Challenge in this context does not mean the head to head confrontation which is frequently (and unfortunately) associated with the word. Rather it encompasses challenge in the way the word is used by athletes, that is, setting a new challenge or goal for which to strive, the challenge to improve and to do better. At times people do this for themselves and at times one needs direct input, feedback and direction from another.

Being challenged is part of the process of professional practice and it is important that it is reflected in an open, honest and questioning culture. Structures need to be in place which provide for challenge in a positive and proactive way.

Working in environments which deal with the pain, distress or emotional needs of others can be demanding and draining on practitioners. They need opportunities to re-charge their batteries, thereby maintaining their objectivity and focus in carrying out a responsible and worthwhile job.

Ultimately, Support in Supervision contributes to all of this and as such plays a significant part in ensuring quality practice by professionals.

It is important to remember that in any organisation ...

*Supervision is about more than Support and*
*Support comes from more places than Supervision*

# Learning

The learning function in Supervision relates to Learning in its widest context and includes self awareness, insight and understanding as well as acquiring knowledge and developing skills. Learning encompasses becoming informed regarding organisational policies and procedures, being aware of professional standards and discovering alternate ways to deal with situations. Above all, learning in Supervision is about becoming more self aware and insightful regarding what you do and how you do it. It is about developing awareness regarding what motivates you in the work, what attracted you into the particular work in the first place and what keeps you in it long after the initial motivation has altered.

However, Learning in Supervision is about more than the Learning for the individual. When incorporated effectively, the Learning encompasses the organisation as a whole and can contribute to service development.

The benefits to the organisation or service can only be fully realised when the culture is one of openness and accountability; when everyone in the organisation is expected to reflect on what is going on and question and learn from each other, and when the structures which facilitate development are applied to all those employed in the organisation and not just to those recently recruited or to those in certain positions. Active curiosity, which is encouraged and channelled, ignites learning for both the individual and for the organisation.

Writing in 1991 Easterby-Smith et al stated that

> "Knowledge can be acquired by reading and talking or by attending courses, skills can be acquired through practising them in either a simulated or a real environment and personal qualities can be acquired through life or educational experiences."

Gaining knowledge, acquiring new skills, developing further insight and becoming more self aware is not just the prerogative of the new recruit - it is vital for professionals at all stages of their career, regardless of their level of experience and responsibility within the workplace.

> "We can always learn and do better, no matter how well we think we are doing at present, "good enough" is not good enough, we always need to be striving to do even better"
>
> (Pedler et al 1997)

## Interdependence of the Three Functions of Supervision

It is important to remember that the three functions of Supervision are interdependent and that very seldom will the task of Supervision fall exclusively into any one of these areas.

While stressing the importance of ensuring balance, over time, in Supervision between the three components - accountability, support and learning - it is also necessary to remember that there may be times in a particular Supervision meeting when the supervisor needs to focus more on one aspect of the three components than the others. For example, in response to a particular difficulty or upset the emphasis may need to be on providing immediate support to the supervisee with a view to subsequently re-focusing at a later time on the learning to be gained for future practice.

Even when the emphasis of a particular meeting is, by necessity, on one component, the supervisor still needs to keep the other components in mind and be aware of their role and responsibilities within the supervisory process. The supervisor at all times holds responsibility for ensuring that each component of the supervisory process is not overlooked. So, although the supervisee may need immediate support s/he is still accountable for practice and will benefit from further insight and learning from the situation for the future. The supervisor must keep this in mind and take the steps necessary to facilitate the overall process.

If, over a number of Supervision meetings, the focus is regularly on the same component, then, being aware of this, the supervisor needs to take responsibility for addressing it. This can be achieved either by acknowledging it to the supervisee to consider the possible reasons and ways of addressing it or alternatively, the supervisor may need to change their approach or style of supervising. If an imbalance is evident over a number of Supervision meetings then the supervisor will also need to reflect on the dynamic which may be contributing to this and explore their own motivation and responsibilities in the process. In either case, the onus is on the supervisor to be self aware and to make conscious decisions regarding the focus and input required in the Supervision process at any one time.

The interrelationship between such accountability, support and learning is the key to facilitating professional Supervision which is effective for all involved - the supervisee, the supervisor, the service and ultimately the people who use the services through improved quality care and service delivery.

The supervisor who understands and fully integrates each of these components throughout the supervisory process is likely to ensure effective professional Supervision.

*Support without learning becomes a crutch*
*Accountability without support is just "check-listing"*
*Learning without accountability does not necessarily lead to improved practice at either individual or organisational level.*

# *Dual Focus Approach*

Anecdotal evidence suggests that the experience of many practitioners has been that, if provided, Supervision has focused on either one of two things. It has focused on ensuring that certain work or tasks were carried out and on planning for what needed to happen next. This leads to Supervision being driven by procedures and checking standards and compliance. This focuses on the Operational aspects of one's role and is necessary in ensuring a level of accountability. However, this does not always take account of the person carrying out the work. The other way in which some practitioners have experienced Supervision is that it has focused on themselves as individuals without considering the context of the work. This can be supportive of the individual and can at times bring about an increased level of self awareness. This in itself is valuable, but does not always consider the needs and outcomes for the client group or ensure the accountability of practice in which all Professional Supervision must take place.

This suggests that Supervision of all practitioners - whether working in community settings or in in-patient or residential care settings and whether for students, experienced practitioners or for managers - will benefit from considering a *Dual Focus Approach.* This will ensure an Operational and a Developmental Focus (O Neill 2000).

The Operational Focus is centred on the Task of the work and on the tasks of the specific role and responsibilities of the individual. One way of introducing this is to consider the job description of the supervisee and to explore their specific responsibilities. While the Operational Focus is on the

Task and tasks of the work, the Developmental Focus is based on the person who carries out the Task and tasks. This ensures attention to the person, thereby facilitating their greater self awareness and objectivity.

Examples of areas to be considered in both the Operational and Developmental aspects can be seen in Figure 2.

*Figure 2.*

## Dual Focus Approach

| **Operational Focus** | **Developmental Focus** |
|---|---|
| *This focus is on the overall **Task** of the Role and on the tasks of the job.* *The job to be done.* | *This focus is on the individual **Person** carrying out the Task and tasks.* *The supervisees themselves.* |
| **Examples include:** | **Examples include:** |
| • The overall purpose and function of the service<br>• Job description<br>• The role of the individual<br>• Policies and procedures<br>• The client group<br>• Assessing needs<br>• Care plans / Key work<br>• Work/Shift planning<br>• Time Management<br>• Recording and report writing<br>• Budgeting /Funding<br>• Staffing / Recruitment<br>• Service planning | • The impact of the work on the person<br>• The individual's strengths and skills<br>• Areas which require improvement and further development<br>• Working as a team member<br>• Recognition and use of one's own support system<br>• Reflection on input, ideas and concerns<br>• Formulating, implementing and evaluating a professional development plan (PDP). |

It is important to bear in mind that
> "If Supervision is focused on practice in isolation to its context it contributes to the system remaining closed." (Corcoran 1999).

The context in which Supervision takes place is the work and the context of the work should be based on the needs of the specific client group.

To successfully implement a Dual Focus Approach it is necessary to understand the direct and indirect connections between each. While these are two independent aspects of the model, it is their interdependence which leads to the most effective use of the process. Overlap must exist to ensure that the functions of Accountability, Support and Learning, are met. The supervisor who understands this will integrate the two foci throughout the Supervision process to the benefit of the supervisee with direct impact for those using the service.

The following brief examples indicate connections between the *Operational and Developmental aspects of the Dual Focus Approach*

- The supervisee who is undertaking key-working for the first time may present in Supervision with a list of questions seeking information and direction. His/her objective is clear - find out what to do so that he/she can begin the task of key-working. The supervisor can respond in a number of different ways. She can provide the answers and give specific directions ... thereby taking charge/responsibility for the work of the supervisee *(operational focus)* She can check out with the supervisee his/her ideas regarding the task in hand and drawing on this can consider options for the work within agreed procedures and identified needs. She can acknowledge the existing skills and experiences of the supervisee and discuss the areas which will require further development in order for him/her to engage in effective keywork *(developmental focus)*.

- The Cook in a Probation Hostel may be highly qualified and experienced as a chef. The setting in which they now work may be totally new to them. So, although familiar with the task for which they are employed they may also be totally unprepared for the complexities of working in the probation hostel. This is where the supervisor needs to facilitate discussion on the impact of being employed to cook (a familiar task) in the new environment (unfamiliar setting). In this context it is not sufficient for the supervisor to focus solely on the supervisees cooking abilities *(operational focus)*. She must also focus on the setting and ensure that attention is paid to the possible or actual impact of the environment on the person *(developmental focus)*.

- The nurse, who is upset by her first involvement with a young patient who is terminally ill may present in Supervision seeking to feel better about her reactions to this traumatic situation. If, however, Supervision is only used as a means of doing this, it will not have fulfilled its proper function. In Supervision this nurse should be supported to reflect on her experiences and to be accountable for her practices *(operational focus)*. She should also be facilitated to develop her awareness of self in practice and to further develop her skills around this area of professional development *(developmental focus)*.

To effectively work from a *Dual Focus Approach* the supervisor must fully understand and have the ability to integrate the operational and developmental foci.

Implementing a *Dual Focus Approach* is best achieved in an organisational climate and culture which is open - open to learning, open to change and open to difference. It requires a commitment - on behalf of the agency and of the supervisor - to the standard of service to those who use it and to the individual practitioner. It requires the commitment of each supervisee to engage in a meaningful and proactive way to ensure the standard and quality of their practice.

Supervision which balances both an *Operational* and a *Developmental Focus* in an integrated manner will ensure its effective use. Used in this way, Supervision is a process of communication and facilitation which supports and equips staff to fulfil their responsibilities to required standards and to further develop their skills and self awareness as reflective practitioners.

# *Induction, Appraisal and their links with Professional Supervision*

Retaining competent workers is a key consideration in managing the human resources in many organisations. At times of high staff turnover and increased job opportunities in many sectors, it is vital that organisations pay particular attention to structures which allow staff to feel recognised and valued. This can enhance their level of job satisfaction and maintain motivation, both of which impact on the quality of service provided as well as on the retention of competent staff.

Induction, Supervision and Appraisal (also referred to as Performance Reviews) are each recognised as valuable structures in supporting the human resources of many organisations. Although each of the three components is distinct and has a specific function, they are also interrelated. When used effectively, they combine to provide a comprehensive means to facilitate and ensure the ongoing accountability, growth and development of the individual and of the service.

**Induction** is the process by which the agency assists the new post holder to become familiar with the job in the context of the policies, procedures and practice.

**Appraisal** is the mechanism to ensure that staff development and organisational goals are met through review of performance and the setting of objectives at periodic intervals.

A system that encompasses each of the three components Induction, Professional Supervision and Appraisals and at the same time ensures effective linkages between them, will maximise the benefits

(a) to the client group - by ensuring safe, relevant, quality care and service to meet their needs

(b) to the staff - by providing a supportive, challenging environment in which they can develop their potential as professionals

(c) to the service - by facilitating a culture of accountability, openness and growth to meet the ever-changing needs of rapidly developing practice.

With increased recognition of the need to consider the ongoing development of staff at all stages of their career there is greater demand on employers and managers to provide efficient methods to ensure the continued development of staff in an effective way.

The idea that qualification is an end in itself has, in recent times, been replaced with a firm belief in the importance of ongoing development and lifelong learning. Gone is the era when graduation marked the pinnacle of ones formalised learning. Today, basic qualification is viewed as a point of entry to many professions. Promotion is frequently dependent on further studies and integration of learning as well as on the experience and potential of the individual.

This shift in expectations contributes to the need for recognised structures in the workplace to facilitate ongoing learning and integration of such learning (formal and informal) to practice.

Connecting theory **to** practice is recognised as a central component of placement experience for student; assimilating learning **from** practice should be an expected component in the ongoing development of all practitioners and ultimately can provide a proactive approach to organisation learning and development.

## Induction and the link to Professional Supervision

Induction to the workplace and to the role and responsibilities for all new staff is recognised as central in equipping people to carry out their professional task. However, Induction can mean a variety of things in different organisations. The immediate pressure of the workplace often dictates this and is particularly evident at times of staff shortages and crises. This can contribute to newly recruited or newly promoted staff being thrown in at the deep end and expected to get on with it - the sink or swim approach.

Induction plays a key role in ensuring that the individual's knowledge, skills and potential, which were identified during the recruitment and selection process, are given the opportunity to become integrated into their role and responsibilities. It allows time for new staff to become familiar with the necessary operational procedures and practices within the service and to develop as team members.

The importance of Induction for all newly appointed post holders, and not just for those new to the organisation, is recognised. Marsh and Triseliotis (1996) identify the importance of Induction in the context of those working in Probation and Social Work. Writing in 1992, Skinner suggested that Induction training, equivalent to two working weeks, should be given priority above all other forms of training for staff. Some may feel that the equivalent to two working weeks is a luxury not always readily available in today's climate of staff shortages and frequent turnover. However the time invested in Induction training can pay rich dividends as the new recruit becomes a competent worker.

Induction takes many forms in different organisations and, even with the best planning and commitment, can at times be influenced by the immediate needs of the service. Such needs may dictate that Induction is a mere passing on of the most basic and necessary information for the new post holder to "get through the day" with the intention of spending "more time when things quieten down". Unfortunately for many, things do not quieten down and the new member of the team learns how to muddle through dependent on their own instincts, ideas or past experiences. In such circumstances it is no surprise that practice often develops in an ad-hoc, reactive and inconsistent manner.

Alternately, Induction in some services is comprehensive, well structured and time related with clear objectives. It may involve the new member shadowing an experienced person for a period of time while they get to know the locations, personnel and policies necessary to become independent practitioners.

Comprehensive Induction will provide new members of the team with both the information necessary to do the job and opportunities to consider their understanding within the context of their experiences. The latter can be achieved through regular Supervision with a designated person. This is more effective if it develops over time, thus allowing the new post holder to reflect on the reality of their work rather than on unrealistic or idealistic expectations which can frequently be a feature of the early days on the job for many people.

Some of the larger organisations now take a two-strand approach to Induction encompassing Corporate or Service Induction and Job or Task Specific Induction. It is frequently the latter which is linked to Supervision and very often the first three to six months of a new job will require a concentrated input which complements the formal Induction.

Supervision in the early days of a new job needs to allow for discussion of some areas already covered in the formal Induction to ensure that the information received has been processed and thus integrated into practice. Opportunities to question and seek clarification regarding aspects of the new role and responsibilities need to be facilitated in Supervision. Following the formal Induction, new workers may well have acquired significant relevant information concerning policies and procedures but it is vital that they also have the opportunity to consider the practice implications of such information. It is necessary for the supervisor and manager to be satisfied that the new worker has gained a sufficient grasp of the specifics of the new working environment to carry out their responsibilities effectively.

The link between Induction and Supervision is apparent when a clear plan exists which outlines the objectives for the new worker for the first week, the first month and the first three to six months. To allow for this, the frequency of Supervision meetings is usually greater during this time than later on. This can correspond to the probationary period, at the end of which, if successful, the worker is deemed competent and their permanence in the job is usually confirmed.

Time and resources invested at this level can make the difference between staff becoming confused, overwhelmed and even disheartened or developing into valuable members of the service who possess a deeper understanding of their role within the context of the organisation. This process does not happen overnight, it requires planning, input and commitment through structured Supervision which provides direction, regular feedback and time for reflection.

## Appraisal and the Link to Professional Supervision

In the business sector, Performance Reviews or Appraisals are acknowledged and used as a means of ensuring staff development and effective and efficient service delivery. However, until recently, they have been frequently absent in many Health Care settings. Appraisals, when used as part of an overall staff development framework, become a proactive mechanism to provide for the planned and integrated practice and development of each staff member and provide valuable feedback to the organisation as a whole.

Setting objectives for continued development are a significant feature of the Appraisal; however it is important to be realistic in the number and type of objectives set if they are to be achieved. The preparation for Appraisal by both the appraisee and the appraiser contributes greatly to its value. It can mean the difference between a proactive process which benefits both participants and the service or a meeting of form filling and going through the motions.

Appraisals which happen in isolation to the ongoing work of the individual are of limited use and have been experienced as little more than an added pressure by many people. A tangible connection to ongoing practice must be apparent to ensure the benefits of Appraisals. A framework which encompasses Induction, Professional Supervision and Appraisal, will ensure that the benefits of each are fully integrated into tangible practice.

*Figure 3*

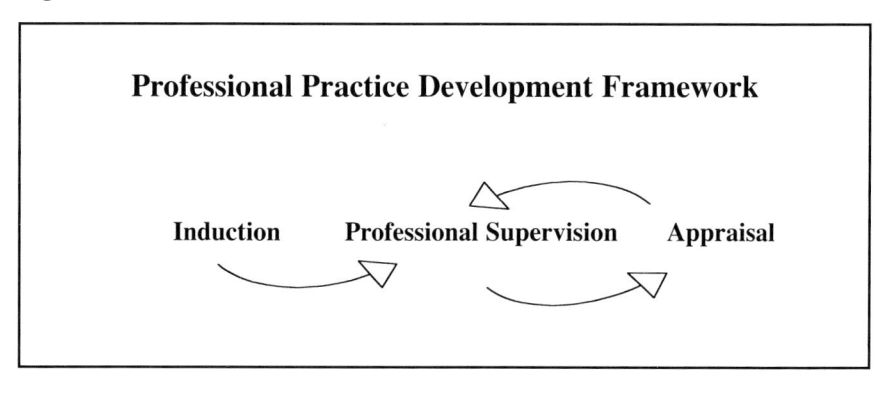

**Professional Practice Development Framework**

Induction     Professional Supervision     Appraisal

When such a framework exists: Induction is incorporated into early Supervision, some aspects of Supervision link to the Appraisal and objectives set in the Appraisal inform part of the ongoing Supervision agenda. This allows for the integration of learning and can thus facilitate improved practice.

## *Who Needs Supervision?*

Reference is made to the Supervision needs and requirements of a range of practitioners, by professional bodies, government reports, and recommendations from a significant number of inquiry reports. (See Part 1)

Supervision is generally seen as part of practice for those working directly in the wider Social Services and Health Sector. It could be said however that the benefits of effective Supervision are applicable to anyone whose work involves a requirement for Accountability, Support and Learning. This is particularly so when that work involves them in regular and direct contact with the public in receipt of services provided by, or on behalf of, the state.

General Practitioners (GPs), Fire and Ambulance personnel, Prison Officers and members of the Gardai are among others who immediately come to mind as having acute needs for regular, structured arrangements for ongoing Professional Supervision as it is outlined here. Their work brings them into daily contact, in an intense and frequently pressurised way, with those who need and often depend on the services provided. Practitioners in these areas are on the receiving end of the distress, trauma and at times hostility of others and often their work is carried out in the public eye. Members of the clergy also work under such pressure, in equally demanding circumstances. Those whose ministry is carried out in parishes frequently do so in isolation to their colleagues, increasingly without a readily available support structure to help them cope with the pressures they can experience on a daily basis, thus contributing to a lonely working environment for some.

Working as all of these people do, requires tangible support structures. Changing environments with new legislation and guidelines, and a greater public expectation of accountability, all contribute to the need for ongoing learning, reflection and feedback through regular, formal structures and input.

Supervision of supervisors is essential. All those with responsibility for the Supervision of others need to ensure that they are actively engaged in effective Supervision for themselves. Without it, their objectivity can become clouded and thus they can contribute to unhealthy processes in the supervisory partnership with their supervisees.

The following provides two examples of those who would benefit from participation in regular formal Supervision in two different settings in the wider health and social care sector - one a multidisciplinary Community Care team and the other a Residential Child Care service.

## *Multidisciplinary Community Care Team*

The range of professions represented in a multidisciplinary team can be vast. As well as their responsibilities within their own profession, they must also practice within a wider context and understanding in order to contribute to a holistic approach to service delivery. All those involved in such a team need ongoing, formal Supervision to ensure that they contribute productively and effectively to the work of the service and to consider the "fit" between their roles and the process of teamwork.

- Social Workers: among a range of their responsibilities, Social Workers play a key role in the decision making process in child protection cases for which they hold statutory responsibility.
- Child Care Workers: the evolving role of the Community Child Care Worker can lead to confusion in some teams regarding their specific responsibilities. They work intensely with young people and with families in family homes, in community settings and at times in public places to meet specific needs.

- The Public Health Nurses: often the first point of contact for many families in their own home and working alone in such settings can add to vulnerability for practitioners.
- Psychologists: the future service needs and provision for the client, are strongly dependent on the assessment focus of the Psychologist's role.
- Administration Staff: these are frequently the first people that many of those accessing the services speak to or meet on arrival. Their responsibilities are significant in dealing with contacts to the services.
- Team: combined with the individual supervisory needs of each of the members of the multidisciplinary team in their own role, the needs of the team as a whole must also be considered. This ensures the best use of the available resources and minimises overlaps or gaps in service provision. It also addresses the process of team working with such diverse experiences and expectations as those found in a multidisciplinary team. This ultimately can lead to more relevant and seamless service provision.

## *Residential Child Care Service*

Working in Residential Care services demands much from the practitioner, who needs to be totally aware of the complexities and demands of working in such an environment. Self awareness is a core requirement for effective practice in this setting.

All staff involved in the care and protection of young people in care and those in regular contact with them through their work should receive regular, formal Supervision. This includes:

- Care staff: their primary focus is direct contact with the young people.
- Managers/directors: their involvement directly and indirectly impacts on the life of the young people.
- Relief staff: they may not be part of a particular team but are nonetheless expected to be involved in direct contact with the young people, often at times of staff shortages or crises.
- Social Workers, psychologists, play therapists and others who are

employed to work directly in and with the residential service.
- Housekeeping and maintenance staff: they may have daily contact with the young people.
- On site teachers: they may work in isolation to their colleagues on a one to one basis with a child.
- Students on placement.
- All those providing Supervision to others: Supervision for the supervisor is essential and a prerequisite for all good Supervision.
- Team: Coupled with the needs of all of the above as individuals, is the need for Supervision of the Team. Residential care is provided in a group setting for young people and staff are expected to work as members of a team. It therefore follows that some Supervision is necessary which focuses on the group and on the team process as well as on the practitioner as an individual.

Supervision is not just for practitioners at certain stages of their career or in certain roles within an organisation. It should be an expected part of practice in which all participate, regardless of their level of experience or seniority within the organisation. (See more under *Myths* page 45-52 and *Commitment* page 57-59)

# *Myths*

A number of myths exist concerning Supervision. These myths need to be explored and indeed exploded before the practice of Professional Supervision can become a positive reality for practitioners at all stages of their professional development. Such myths are frequently fundamental to the blocks experienced by many in the Supervisory process.

### *Myth: " Everyone knows what Supervision is"*
This is a myth, not a fact. There are many different interpretations of what Supervision is. These interpretations are frequently based on the present role of the individual and or on their past experiences of receiving or not receiving Supervision.

For Supervision to be provided and used effectively as a positive resource within any organisation, there must be a shared and agreed understanding of what is meant by Professional Supervision in the context of the discipline.

Taking for granted that those entering work share a common understanding of Supervision is unrealistic and unfair and places the Supervisory process at a disadvantage from the beginning. Students entering the workplace do so with a variety of expectations regarding Supervision. This can depend on the college they attended or on early placement experience or even on what they have been told or picked up from fellow students or friends. Some students see Supervision as a test or exam - this should not be the case - like all Supervision it should be seen as an opportunity for growth and learning, a forum to receive support and to ensure accountable practice.

Experienced practitioners entering a new agency or service will also be influenced by their earlier experiences of Supervision, or lack of them. They may be coming from a background where Supervision was associated with problems or only provided following a crisis or compulsory only for young or inexperienced practitioners. On the other hand they may have had very positive experiences of Supervision and be looking forward to it, although somewhat apprehensive about beginning with a new Supervisor.

Clarity regarding the purpose and function of professional Supervision, the responsibilities of both the supervisor and supervisee and of how Supervision is prioritised and carried out within the organisation, are fundamental to ensuring a common understanding and approach for effective Supervision.


## *Myth:"Everyone wants or welcomes Supervision"*

In reality this is not true. It is important to remember that

- Reservations are normal
- Anxieties are common
- Resistance is not unusual

Supervision has been described by Graham as *"a reflective process through which professionals enhance their personal and professional development"*(1994).

The idea of entering a reflective process on either an individual basis or in a group context is perceived as a risky experience for many people.

*"What if the Supervisor thinks I can't do the job or thinks I'm not coping?"*

*"I'm new here, - I better prove that I can do this job."*

*"Will it be seen as a sign of weakness if I use or look for Supervision?"*

These are some of the thoughts that can impinge on how Supervision is perceived and used in any organisation. Supervisors need to be sensitive to the real issues that can exist for those entering Supervision, particularly in the early stages. Rather than seeing the reservations and anxieties as a difficulty, the skilled supervisor respects and accepts them as part of what the person may bring to Supervision and works with them.

Resistance is not uncommon from some staff who may have worked for many years without any formal Supervision and may see its introduction as a threat or a questioning of their competence rather than as the positive resource it can be. She or he may feel confused or threatened by the supervisor with whom they have worked as a colleague for years and who has now been given supervisory responsibility. On the other hand, if the Supervisor is newly appointed to the service, s/he may be perceived as too new/young/inexperienced by the practitioner of many years' standing. Supervision is a process and must be allowed time to develop, particularly when newly introduced to a service.

## *Myth: " Only young or new staff need Supervision."*

This is a myth, which has had damaging effects on how Supervision has been perceived and used in many agencies. The need for Supervision does not lessen with experience, although the use made of it can change at different stages of one's development. Experience suggests that increased responsibility can in fact indicate a greater need for effective Supervision as the forum for gaining support, learning and accountability can lessen. The isolation often experienced by some senior staff, managers and directors is evidence of this.

The culture of the organisation must provide an expectation that all staff from the most senior to the newest student on placement participate in regular, formal Professional Supervision. Participation in Supervision should be an expected and accepted part of practice at all levels of responsibility for all those engaged in professional practice at all stages of their career.

*Myth: "Anyone can supervise"*

This has been a common myth which has led to Supervision often being provided in an ad hoc fashion, at times by those ill-equipped or unprepared to do so. Frequently the responsibility for supervising students and staff has been imposed on people with little if any consideration given either for their already pressurised workload or their level of skill and competence to carry out such a task.

For Professional Supervision to be effective, it should be provided by Supervisors who have specific skills and training coupled with a keen understanding of the role and function of professional Supervision and an appreciation of the particular discipline.

For example, those supervising staff in a residential child care setting need to value the unique role residential care plays in the lives of young people and understand the complexities and dynamics of sharing their living space while maintaining professional boundaries at all times.

All students, on completion of their qualifying courses, should have obtained knowledge on the theory and practice of Supervision in order to understand and appreciate its role and function in professional practice. This will ensure that those entering the workplace do so with an informed understanding of Professional Supervision and are aware of their responsibilities for its effective use. On entering the workplace newly qualified staff should have an expectation that Professional Supervision will be provided as part of their employment. However, to effectively provide Professional Supervision demands considerably more than knowledge about the topic. Knowledge about Supervision should not be confused with the skill of supervising.

To provide effective Supervision for others demands an experienced practitioner with highly developed interpersonal skills who is self aware and has developed their ability to facilitate others to reflect on their practice in a manner that is affirming, supportive and at the same time challenging.

Experienced professionals, whose work involves the Supervision of others, need specialised training at post-qualifying level to equip them for this task. *"Training is an essential part in the development of supervisors and must include attention to expanding their knowledge, developing skills and exploring attitudes."* (O Neill 2000). It is not enough for supervisors to have only an academic grasp of the subject. Supervisors need to have a keen understanding and appreciation of all aspects of the practice and process of Supervision; they need to have developed insight and self awareness coupled with specific skills. (See Page ?? in Part Two for more on the specific skills necessary for the effective supervisor). Supervision for the supervisor is another essential requirement in ensuring effective Supervision. There is no replacement for receiving good Supervision and without it supervisors should not be providing Supervision for others.

## *Myth: "Supervision is nothing more than a talking-shop, nothing changes"*

This comment is used at times to describe Supervision by those who have not fully considered the purpose and function of Professional Supervision and who do not appreciate the responsibilities inherent in the supervisory partnership. Those with such opinions may never have experienced effective Supervision themselves. Expecting Supervision on its own to bring about change, either in the work environment or in the practice of individuals, without due consideration for the culture of the organisation, the ability of the staff or the overall responsibilities of Supervisee, Supervisor and service is unfair on all concerned and indeed an unrealistic and mistaken interpretation of Professional Supervision. Based on a shared understanding and common objectives within a service, Professional Supervision provides a structure for accountable, quality practice, which is at the core of the delivery of professional practice in any organisation or discipline.

## Myth: "Supervision is only about problems"

Again this comment indicates a limited understanding regarding the real meaning of Professional Supervision and can inhibit its use in some organisations. If Supervision is associated with problems only, then it is likely that there will be resistance to its being used as an effective and positive resource in a proactive way to benefit all involved, indirectly and directly; this includes those who use the services as well as those who work in the services.

The overall culture of the service or organisation will quickly indicate whether Supervision is perceived as "problem only" or seen as a "proactive resource". If the latter is the norm there will be evidence in the regularity and structure of Supervision and in the infrequency of cancelled appointments. The agenda as well as the meetings will be planned for, with regular input from both supervisee and supervisor. "Problem only" Supervision, on the other hand, is more often associated with infrequent and unplanned meetings only, which focus on a narrow agenda usually related to the most recent or immediate crisis or problem.

Notwithstanding this, it is important to reiterate here that, as well as being regularly available in a scheduled manner for all, Professional Supervision should also be available at times of particular difficulty or crisis for individuals at their request or if the Supervisor identifies a need. Such Supervision needs to be seen and used as extra and not take over from the regular, planned meetings.

Professional Supervision includes attention to problem areas but if used effectively it is also about so much more. It encompasses self awareness, areas of interest, ongoing professional development, affirmation, details regarding practice, skills use and development as well as, already mentioned, accountable practice, support and overall learning.

## *Myth: Supervision is a waste of time and resources*

This is a myth which may be held on to by those who have never fully participated in effective Supervision themselves or who have not had the opportunity to consider the role and function of professional Supervision in an organisational and individual context.

Supervision requires a time commitment and professionals with the capacity to deliver quality Supervision for others. However, if attention is paid to the structure and process of providing Supervision in the agency/service then there is far less likelihood of a waste of valuable resources. On the contrary, providing regular and structured time with a clear agenda in the context of known roles and responsibilities can in fact minimise time-wasting in other situations. For example, outside of Supervision the casual use of the interruption "have you got a minute?" which can drag into several minutes and more, can be lessened when both know that there is a scheduled meeting coming up which can deal with the issue.

Supervision needs to have an identified and allocated time span; the time available should not be open-ended. A prearranged and well structured hour, for which both supervisee and supervisor come prepared and knowing what is expected of them, is productive. If, however, Supervision time is spent drifting through discussion aimlessly or trying to cram in topics it will not be effective, regardless of the duration of the session.

Supervisors who are aware of, and comfortable with, the purpose and function of Supervision within their role and within the service, are more inclined to ensure the effective use of the time available than those who are unsure and unclear of what is required.

To ensure effective use of Supervision it is necessary to dispel the many myths that exist. This will be achieved through initial discussion and exploration of what is meant by effective Professional Supervision and by attention to the development of the skills necessary for its purposeful and responsible implementation. A policy that is realistic and is realistically carried out is another factor which will ensure that effective purposeful Supervision is a reality. A shared understanding and meaning of effective Supervision must replace the myths which exist. Only then will Supervision become the positive and proactive resource it can be.

---

*Part One has considered the need for Professional Supervision and outlined what Supervision is not as well as what it is. It has explored its functions of accountability, support and learning. A Dual Focus approach which is based on both the task (operational focus) and the person in the task (developmental focus) was considered. The need for Supervision within certain work settings and disciplines were introduced. Links between Supervision, Induction and Performance Appraisal were outlined and finally part one sought to explode some of the myths surrounding professional Supervision.*

*Part Two focuses on the factors necessary for the introduction and implementation of Professional Supervision for the individual practitioner and for the organisation as a whole. It considers the criteria necessary for the development and operation of a service policy on Professional Supervision. The factors necessary to promote the delivery and participation of Supervision between the partners in the process are outlined and skills necessary for effective Supervision are explored. The reality of Supervision is highlighted for two practitioners and some frequently asked questions are considered under the heading What if...?*

# *Professional Supervision*

## *Myths, Culture and Structure*

### *Part 2*

# *Providing Effective Supervision*

In considering the introduction of Supervision to a service or discipline, significant benefit will be gained from some attention to the overall, long-term objectives as well as to its specific and immediate aims. The same applies when reframing existing Supervision within an organisation. Professional Supervision demands the support and realistic commitment of senior management in any organisation to be effective. Its introduction or redevelopment in services needs to be thought through in terms of expectations, capacity to deliver and evaluation of practice.

Numerous recommendations have been made on the importance of structured and formal Supervision as part of professional practice. More and more practitioners at all levels of their development are beginning to consider the use of Supervision as a resource to equip them for the ongoing reality of the workplace. Nonetheless, it is vital that each organisation and discipline considers the purpose and function of Supervision within their own context. They should subsequently develop a realistic structure, within agreed guidelines, which best meets their specific needs.

Establishing effective Supervision in organisations requires attention to a range of factors. When initiating change it is important that a clear vision exists of what will be different following the change. It is beneficial if the reason for the change, and what is required of all involved, is understood. This suggests viewing the introduction of Supervision as a process not merely as an event.

Hawkins (2002) suggested some useful ways of introducing Supervision for the first time. Among these were the need to stimulate enquiry into existing practices and to develop both a comprehensive policy and practice of Supervision. The use of pilot projects allows for guided practice and the time and space to work with overcoming resistance to change. The training and development of supervisors and supervisees is essential at the outset. Any new process or policy introduced into an organisation requires a clear monitoring and evaluation system to be put in place.

For Supervision to be truly effective it needs to:
- be part of the culture of the organisation
- be understood as a process not as an event
- be fully supported by senior management
- facilitate the development of professionally accountable practitioners
- empower the supervisee and ultimately the client
- be practice focused
- facilitate professional objectivity
- contribute to high standards of effective, safe care/service
- encourage reflective practice
- contribute to organisational learning

To ensure that Supervision is effective requires more than just a decision to provide it. A number of key factors need to be considered in the provision of effective Supervision in any organisation or discipline. These include the culture, commitment, capacity and mandate of the organisation.

- **Culture:** The culture of the service will impact on the effectiveness of Supervision and equally effective Supervision can strongly influence the culture of the organisation. Accountability, Support and Learning are the main functions of all Supervision. When these are embedded in the daily fabric of the workplace it provides a safer, more satisfying environment which thus impacts positively on the quality of care and service.

  Providing effective Supervision requires a culture of openness, accountability and transparency within the organisation - openness to change, openness to difference, accountability for omissions as well as for actions and transparency regarding practice and processes. It is within such an atmosphere that Supervision can be truly effective.

Establishing and maintaining a culture of openness in an organisation is not as simple as it may sound. The "hidden culture" as opposed to the "purported culture" is very often what informs the attitudes and subsequent behaviours in many organisations. Being told of the policy during induction and subsequently discovering from colleagues that the practice is in fact significantly different, provides mixed messages. Such mixed messages often confuse and at times disempower the newly appointed staff member. Furthermore, mixed messages undermine accountability within the workplace and subsequently destabilise the Supervision process before it even gets started.

Culture has been described in a number of ways by various writers. Ouchi and Johnson (1978) describe culture as *"how things are done around here"*. Braten (1983) said culture is *"the way of thinking, speaking and (inter)acting that characterise a certain group"* Therefore the culture is influenced by all those involved in an organisation and can therefore be changed, for better or worse, by the people of the organisation.

The components of effective Supervision - Accountability, Support and Learning - need to be firmly valued and established in the overall culture of any organisation if Supervision is to be used as a positive and constructive resource. Training of supervisors is more likely to be effective when it includes focus on and challenges the cultural dimension of the service.

- **Commitment:** The commitment to Supervision must be apparent within the organisation - this means it must be prioritised and recognised as valuable and necessary by both management and staff alike.

1. Evidence of commitment to Supervision in any organisation can be seen where the Director or Senior Manager is actively engaged in receiving regular, effective Supervision for themselves. Expecting staff to participate in Supervision but not the managers is giving mixed messages; it implies that they have no need for it. The need for accountability, support and continued learning do not end when someone gets a senior position; the need can in fact become greater as one takes on more responsibility. Increased responsibility and seniority in many organisations can lead to greater isolation which in itself indicates the need for structured arrangements for ensuring accountability of practice, accessing effective support and maintaining development and further learning. This ensures that managers not only remain up to date with current thinking and developments but that they receive feedback on their overall input to the organisation and receive constructive challenge surrounding aspects of practice which could be further improved and developed. Furthermore many managers find such a process, and the opportunity it provides for self-reflection, extremely beneficial in light of the extreme pace at which they regularly work. No one is so good that there is not some aspect of their practice or process of working that would not benefit from further improvement.

2. The commitment to the practice of Supervision is also apparent in the manner in which participants prepare for and accept responsibility for their Supervision. Beginning the arranged meeting on time, contributing to the agenda in a proactive manner through preparation and reflection, taking responsibility for ensuring that any decisions made are carried through, are some indicators of commitment to the practice of Professional Supervision.

3. The commitment to the process of Supervision on the other hand, is evident in organisations where Supervision is ongoing

and regular, where the style and approach to Supervision develop over time and reflect the ongoing development of the supervisee and where there is an appreciative enquiry into the function and use of Supervision for both the individual and for the organisation.

4. Another indication of commitment to both the practice and process of Supervision is in how it is monitored and evaluated. To ensure quality practice, which facilitates quality service, it is necessary to include a means of evaluation. This is one area which has been neglected to a large extent and requires attention. Evaluation is not just about checking up on the frequency and duration of meetings or reviewing the content. Thorough evaluation is about exploring how Supervision is viewed and used by the organisation and by the individuals within the organisation and examining this in the context of its purpose and function. It is about ensuring that those charged with responsibility for the Supervision of others do so while continually developing and expanding their skills, insights and self awareness regarding all aspects of Supervision. It is about making sure that learning is integrated at organisational level and does not just remain at individual level.

- **Capacity:** The ability within the organisation to provide effective Supervision must be considered and developed. Frequently the responsibility for supervising others is not thought through in the context of the specific ability of the individuals who undertake the task. It has not been unheard of, in the past, for individuals to be given supervisory responsibilities for others without ever having participated in effective Supervision themselves. Some people have had no more preparation for the task than to be told "just meet Mary/Joe and see how s/he is getting on". Is it any wonder then that Supervision has developed in an ad hoc manner, dependent on individual interpretations?

The quality of Supervision is dependent on the ability of the supervisor to facilitate the process which allows for the development of the individual supervisee in a supportive manner while remaining focused on accountable practice. The delivery of effective Supervision in an organisational context demands skilled, insightful supervisors with a strong appreciation of the complexities of the specific work environment who are themselves participating in regular, effective Supervision. Training for the supervisor must take account of attitudes and values as well as skills and knowledge and needs to be understood as a process not as an event.

Organisational capacity to deliver effective Supervision also necessitates consideration of the time and space required within the working environment.

- **Mandate:** An organisational mandate for Supervision will contribute to its effectiveness and ensure that it is viewed and used as a recognised and respected resource for all. The absence of a mandate contributes to Supervision being developed in an ad hoc manner. The need for a mandate is particularly evident in organisations where there is frequent turnover of management which can result in policies and practices being changed with each new post holder. This constant moving of the goal-posts not only leads to insecurity but can also lead to unclear or even unsafe practice. In establishing a mandate, it is incumbent on those charged with overall responsibility to do so, work from an informed understanding of the purpose and function of Professional Supervision with realistic expectations regarding its use and impact.

The mandate of the organisation to provide regular, formal Supervision is apparent in its Supervision Policy. The policy needs to be set within the context of the defined purpose and function of the service and discipline/s. It should provide a clear, realistic, working framework for the use of Supervision, its content and process. The expectations, roles and responsibilities of the three partners involved, i.e. the supervisor, the supervisee and the organisation, must be clearly outlined.

# *Supervision Policy and Procedures*

Policies in all areas of work provide clear statements of what informs the work of the particular organisation, service or discipline. The Procedures detail the factors necessary to implement the policy at practice level. As such, policies and procedures are a way of ensuring that all those involved in the work of the organisation or discipline know what is expected of them in different circumstances. Understanding policies and procedures requires their integration to practice which is achieved through Supervision over time. Well-structured Supervision policy and procedures should provide clarity to the service in general and to the staff members in particular regarding the importance placed on Supervision and on how it will be carried out.

A clear policy on Supervision, which outlines its purpose and states the procedure for Supervision, is essential. As with all Policies, it must be clear and realistic; it must be 'owned' by all those involved in its implementation i.e. by supervisors and supervised and it must be reviewed regularly by the organisation and updated as necessary. The policy should reflect the specific Supervision needs and arrangements of the agency and for this reason it is vital that each organisation or discipline draws up its own Policy and Procedures within recognised guidelines.

The following are among the areas which require consideration in developing Supervision Policy and Procedures in any organisation:

- A statement outlining the mandate for Supervision within the organisation or discipline

- The Purpose and Functions of Supervision within the service or organisation
- Who should receive Supervision and from whom
- Contracting of Supervision
- How Supervision will be carried out
- The content and agenda
- The frequency, duration and location of meetings
- Boundaries regarding confidentiality and the lines of accountability
- Recording - what is recorded, by whom, who has the right to access to the records, where they are kept, for how long and for what they can be used
- What priority is placed on Supervision in relation to other responsibilities and the circumstances which may allow for postponement of a particular meeting
- The procedure in case of difficulties between the supervisee and supervisor
- The rights and responsibilities of the supervisee, the supervisor and of the organisation
- The process for review and evaluation of Supervision

The following factors need to be considered to ensure the structure of Supervision is grounded in realistic objectives and principles:

**Frequency:** Professional Supervision is seen as a regular structured process. The frequency of Supervision will be influenced by professional requirements, individual needs, the stage of development of the supervisee and the service expectations. The frequency varies for different organisations and disciplines between weekly Supervision to meeting once in six weeks.

Whatever the agreed frequency, the provision should also exist for more frequent meetings which may be necessary if the individual, or indeed the organisation, is going through particular changes or difficulties.

It is important that, whatever the agreed time span is, it does not go beyond that except in exceptional circumstances as agreed between the participants. In the event of sickness or an immediate crisis necessitating postponement, then a new appointment must be arranged for as close as possible to the original date.

Working from the belief that Supervision is a process which provides opportunity for the ongoing development of the supervisee as well as ensuring accountable practice, then the formal contact between the partners must be regular and not so spread out that they need to start from scratch each time they meet.

**Duration:** Supervision meetings should have an agreed duration which includes time for the recording of the Supervision meeting. It is the responsibility of both the supervisee and supervisor to ensure that Supervision begins on time. The supervisor is responsible for managing the time during the Supervision meeting and for concluding appropriately and on time.

Whether the allocated time is one hour or more, it is important to adhere to the time agreed. Frequently cutting down on the time given to Supervision minimises its importance and can lead to just 'going through the motions' of providing or attending supervision. Going overtime indicates an undisciplined approach and suggests a supervisor who may be either unsure of their role or is trying to cram everything into Supervision, rather than using other structures for communicating or addressing issues.

A regular, structured prearranged meeting where both people have accepted responsibility for the content is a productive use of valuable resources and does not require excessive time.

**Location:** Supervision is a professional resource and the location of Supervision meetings needs to reflect this. A room free from interruptions and distractions is necessary. The supervisor must ensure that telephones are switched off. A busy office to which others are likely to need access is not a suitable location, nor is the local coffee shop. Accessing a suitable venue is usually the responsibility of the supervisor.

The supervisor who sits behind a desk can give a very different message to the one who sits beside or opposite the supervisee without any physical barrier between them. It is therefore worth considering this in attempting to create a space which is conducive to reflective, honest discussion and feedback.

**Contract:** Ideally the employment contract should include reference to the Supervision requirements within the agency. It is also recommended that a clear Supervision contract or agreement be used between the supervisor and supervisee. This outlines briefly the functions, frequency and duration of Supervision and identifies the responsibilities of both supervisor and supervisee for appointments, agenda, etc. (See appendix 1 for sample of a contract). Ideally the contract is used in conjunction with the organisation's Supervision Policy. The contract needs to be reviewed periodically and updated as the need arises.

**Content:** Supervision is provided to facilitate effective professional practice. To reflect this, the content of Supervision meetings must include attention to the detail of the work and to the individual staff member.

To ensure that Supervision achieves its objectives, a dual focus approach is required i.e. the main focus is two-fold: an *Operational focus* and a *Developmental focus.* The Operational aspect considers the tasks of the work e.g. assessing need, direct care, key-working, recording, relationship building, time management etc. The Developmental aspect considers the person carrying out those tasks i.e. the individual staff member as a person, the impact of work on them, their strengths and areas requiring further development, etc. This facilitates greater self awareness in the staff member and facilitates their ongoing development.

It is worth reiterating that Supervision is not counselling and the supervisor should never get into a situation where they see themselves as a personal counsellor or therapist to the supervisee. If, during Supervision, personal issues are disclosed, which may impact on the work of the supervisee, it may be necessary for the supervisor to refer him or her to a counsellor or to the employee assistance officer in the organisation.

The supervisor must not take on the role of personal counsellor in Supervision. Moore (2000) warns that where the supervisee is engaged in abuse work the Supervision session may drift into a therapy session. The role of the supervisor is not to be a therapist for the supervisee. If this shift occurs it will only blur boundaries and can promote negative future relationships.

Examples of areas for consideration in Supervision are included in Part 1 (pages 18 and 30)

**Agenda:** Planning and preparation for Supervision shows mutual respect between supervisee and supervisor. The agenda is their joint responsibility.

In some situations the agenda is identified in advance of the meeting, while others agree the agenda at the outset of each meeting. Either of these can work, the important aspect here is that there is an agenda, which is identified and agreed at the start of each meeting between the two participants in Supervision.

In some circumstances it may be necessary and valuable to prioritise the agenda at the outset of the meeting, particularly if there is a tendency for Supervision to overrun. This ensures a clearer focus and often a more responsible use of time. Without an agreed agenda, Supervision risks drifting and becoming a "chat" or being focused solely on the most recent event or concern, neither of which reflects the most effective of use Professional Supervision.

Both participants must regularly contribute to the agenda which must reflect the detail of the role and responsibilities of the supervisee.

**Boundaries/**
**Confidentiality:** Confidentiality within Supervision is not absolute. It is the responsibility of the supervisor to appraise the Line Manager of the progress of each staff member and to inform him or her if concerns arise regarding any aspect of the practice of another.

Biestek, writing as far back as 1961 in "The Casework Relationship" highlighted, when considering the sharing of information, the importance of the caseworker's *"implicit understanding that the matter is being communicated not merely to the individual caseworker but also to the agency"*. He went on to explain that the *"caseworker is not a freelance welfare counsellor but an agent of a social agency"*. Likewise the supervisor is not a freelance agent but an agent of the organisation or discipline to which s/he has explicit responsibilities. Within any organisation Supervision is a delegated task and therefore carries with it certain obligations and requirements. Examples of this go beyond concerns regarding the practice of another. It also includes the supervisor needing to bring to their own Supervision aspects of the Supervision they provide. This is necessary for reflection and exploration in order to gain further insights and to ensure accountability for their practice as supervisor as well as for the quality of the Supervision they provide.

In establishing and contracting Supervision, it is necessary that the boundaries and responsibilities, of both the supervisee and the supervisor, regarding the information shared, are clearly outlined and discussed between them. This leads to the process and practice of Supervision being open and honest from the outset.

The aspect of confidentiality within Supervision has been an area of some considerable difference among practitioners and disciplines. This needs to be clarified at the start of the supervisory partnership within the context of agency and/or discipline guidelines.

For some, confusion has existed by Supervision being provided externally to their place of work (but paid for by the employer). This has, for many, taken a counselling dimension which implied total confidentiality. In such situations the supervisee may have experienced considerable support however there has frequently been no link back into the organisation, which has limited the effectiveness of such Supervision for improved practice. Such imbalance in the triangulated components of Supervision needs to be monitored and addressed by the supervisor and by the organisation.

In any professional relationship there are boundaries regarding the sharing of information. How the information is shared, with whom and under what circumstances, are areas requiring clarity. Nonetheless, in the context of a supervisor, within an organisation or agency, delegated to carry out Supervision with another, as part of his or her work, it is imperative that clear lines of reporting are established and understood from the outset by the supervisor, the supervisee and the organisation. Likewise, if Supervision is being provided by a person who does not work for the organisation but is contracted to undertake Supervision on its behalf, the same clarity and detailed obligations apply and need to be incorporated into a contract with commitment to the reporting relationship expected.

**Recording:** Recording of Supervision meetings frequently raises anxiety for many people. *What is being written? Who will see it? Where will it go? What happens if I leave?* These are questions frequently asked and must be clearly and honestly answered with the procedures outlined in the Supervision Policy.

The value of recording is twofold.
Firstly, it provides a framework of accountability for both supervisor and supervisee. Secondly, reviewing records after a certain period of time can prove a valuable learning experience. It can highlight areas of development and change on the one hand or, on the other hand, can indicate gaps or if the same issues are recurring over time. If the latter is the case then they may require a different approach by the supervisor to enable the supervisee to further develop.

It is the responsibility of the supervisor to ensure that a written record is kept of all Supervision meetings. The supervisee should be involved in such recording and with the supervisor signs all records which must be clearly dated. All records must be accessible to the supervisee and available to the line manager as required. A specific recommendation of the Victoria Climbié Inquiry Report stated that *"Directors of Social Services must ensure that senior managers inspect, at least once every three months, a random selection of case files and supervision notes."* (Laming 2003, Recommendation 30)

Supervision records are seen as the property of the employing organisation and as such are subject to the same disclosure conditions and legal requirements as all other professional records.
The record must accurately reflect a summary of the

main points covered and include the detail of any decisions made with a clear indication of who is responsible for carrying them out and, if appropriate, the timescale involved.

Like all professional records, Supervision records should be clearly written, factual, signed and dated. Supervision records do not have to be typed. They must, however, be made contemporaneously and be accessible to the supervisee who should ideally be involved in the recording. Incorporating the recording into the Supervision meeting, where the supervisor and supervisee undertake the recording together in the final stage of each meeting, facilitates this. Recording together further ensures accuracy and immediacy and shared responsibility which adds to the benefits of Supervision.

All Supervision should be recorded on a pro forma sheet which needs to include;
- The names of both supervisor and supervisee
- The Location, Date, Time and Duration of the meeting
- Agenda items with clarity regarding who included what (supervisee or supervisor)
- Any specific responsibilities of the supervisee e.g. key-work, assessment, child protection, staff selection, court reports etc.
- Detail of any decisions made and the responsibilities of each person in carrying them out
- Date and time of next Supervision meeting
- Signatures of both the supervisee and the supervisor - Dated

(See appendix 2 for a sample recording sheet)

**Postponement:** Postponement or cancellations by the supervisor or delayed appointments can cause resentment in the supervisee who had been expecting to receive Supervision and finds their needs are not considered important enough for the appointment to be kept. Regular cancellations can also provide the means for abdication of responsibility by both participants. An example of this is the expectation that both people prepare for Supervision - why prepare if experience has shown that Supervision is more likely not to happen as to happen? There needs to be an explicit statement in the Supervision Policy on what allows Supervision to be postponed, and how, by both the person providing Supervision and the person attending Supervision.

In the event of the absence or illness of the supervisor for a prolonged period of time then an alternative supervisor should be appointed.

**Conflict:** The area of possible conflict with the supervisor is one which can preoccupy many supervisees in a new supervisory partnership. If such a possibility is ignored through silence then it can contribute to tension. By discussing it early on and identifying the steps to be taken if such an event ever occurs, the supervisee frequently feels more at ease and empowered. Furthermore, a service which acknowledges that difficulties can arise and which has considered a means to address such occurrence suggests a culture of openness (as already referred to) and an expectation of accountability with clear responsibility placed on the supervisee, supervisor, line manager and the organisation.

It is important, at an early meeting between the supervisor and new supervisee, that there is discussion on the procedure to be followed in case of difficulties between them. It must also be emphasised that both supervisor and supervisee have mutual responsibility to acknowledge and address such difficulties. If, following this, the difficulty continues then either person (or both) has a responsibility to bring it to the attention of the line manager who will need to consider the means to address the situation. The line manager may meet with both people together or initially individually, always with the intention of working towards the continuation of the original supervisory partnership.

Conflict or difficulties between supervisee and supervisor are not in themselves a reason to terminate the supervisory partnership. The professional response to such a situation is to acknowledge the difficulties and work through them and with them.

Clients do not always have the opportunity to choose who their Social Worker or Probation Officer will be; nevertheless they are expected to work with them to achieve the objectives of the contact. Young people in care do not get to choose who will be on duty at a given time, nor do patients in day or inpatient services, yet they are expected to engage with and accept those who are working with them. Clients of the service are expected to be honest and to work through their difficulties, in what are often much more intense and demanding circumstances. It follows therefore that the professionals providing the services should, at the very least, be expected to do the same.

Practitioners have a responsibility to work together as effectively as possible - this is not to suggest that all practitioners have to like each other. However, as professionals they are expected to find ways of working together for the benefit of those using the services. It may be easier to have the freedom to change supervisor, and indeed supervisee, when the going gets tough, but it is not conducive to honest, responsible practice and is not in keeping with the principles of Professional Supervision. Neither does it contribute to a culture of openness and professional accountability.

Acknowledging and working through difficulties, in the workplace in general and in Supervision in particular, demands committed, honest, professionals who are not prepared to engage in double standards. Engaging pro-actively in a process of working with difficulties can add greatly to the development of both the supervisee and the supervisor. It further enhances the supervisory partnership and ultimately the service provided.

**Ongoing Review:** Regular and formal review of Supervision needs to be inbuilt to the agenda at periodic intervals to ensure that it remains focused on its objectives. The benefits of this include an opportunity for both participants to take responsibility for providing feedback to the other on how each is experiencing Supervision. Provided such feedback is given and heard in an open and honest manner, it can guard against Supervision falling into a comfortable rut or being skewed by the needs or interpretation of either one person or the other.

It can be useful to schedule this review into the agenda approximately every sixth meeting or so. It is not necessary to devote the whole meeting to the review, neither should it just be a nominal check in, e.g. the supervisor asking *"How are you finding Supervision?"* and the supervisee replying *"Fine"* and then moving on to other matters. This is paying lip-service to reviewing Supervision and suggests possible ineffective use of Supervision overall.

Reviewing the supervisory experience requires reflection on aspects which may be proving useful and discussion on what has contributed to this, to ensure greater awareness and ongoing learning for both participants. Identifying areas of disappointment or confusion and considering some of the possible contributory factors are also a valuable focus of the review. Highlighting and exploring recurring issues or themes can be beneficial in ensuring objective awareness to enable future Supervision meetings to move on or address the recurring matters in another way.

There may be other occasions when it is necessary to review Supervision together e.g. if the supervisee regularly limits their agenda to seeking information alone or associates it with problems only.

Many of the responsibilities within the Supervisory partnership are shared between the supervisor and supervisee. Such responsibilities need to be clearly identified and understood from the outset. Below are examples of some of the responsibilities.

| **Supervisory Responsibilities** | Supervisee | Supervisor |
|---|---|---|
| Preparation for Supervision | ✓ | ✓ |
| Starting on time | ✓ | ✓ |
| Finishing on time |  | ✓ |
| Contributing to the agenda | ✓ | ✓ |
| Using the time effectively | ✓ | ✓ |
| Actively listening | ✓ | ✓ |
| Ensuring suitable venue | ✓ | ✓ |
| Ensuring that no interruptions occur (e.g. phones turned off) | ✓ | ✓ |
| Honest communication | ✓ | ✓ |
| Rescheduling postponed meeting | ✓ | ✓ |
| Ensuring accuracy of summary Record and safe keeping of same |  | ✓ |
| Acknowledging difficulties with each other if they arise | ✓ | ✓ |
| Honest communication and feedback | ✓ | ✓ |
| Seeking additional Supervision if necessary | ✓ |  |
| Regular review of Supervision content and process | ✓ | ✓ |

When introducing Supervision to some people or organisations for the first time, it is necessary to consider the following ...

>Are Reservations..................Normal?
>Are Anxieties...................... Usual?
>Is Resistance.................... Unusual?

Reservations, anxieties and resistance are frequently a response to change. They need to be understood by the supervisor and worked with, through Supervision, if they exist.

Having considered factors necessary for the introduction and structure of the Supervision policy and practice in an organisation, the next section further examines structures and skills which facilitate effective Supervision.

# Skills and Tasks of the Supervisor

Effective Supervision requires the use of a range of skills by the supervisor. The skills are similar to those used by the competent practitioner in the course of their work on a daily basis. Examples of these include:

Listening, Observation, Communication,
Reflecting, Challenging, Conflict Management,
Supporting, Affirming, Prompting,
Directing, Informing, Guiding, Assessment,
Questioning, Problem-solving, Leadership,
Feedback, Mediation and Time Management.

## Insightful Self Awareness

Self awareness is when all the senses combine in awareness so that you are present to yourself. Self awareness is a fundamental requirement in all supervisors. It demands constant attention so that it contributes in a conscious and meaningful way to the process and skill of facilitating effective Supervision. This ensures that Supervision is more likely to remain objective and focused on its principles of improved practice and service delivery by the supervisee.

To continue to develop one's self-awareness requires ongoing opportunities for focused self-reflection and challenge. The supervisor receives this from their own Supervision as well as from working in an atmosphere of critical reflection and constructive feedback.

To combine this ability to be present to yourself while simultaneously being present to another in the supervisory process is what is needed in the effective supervisor. To do all of this while remaining in tune with an organisational and disciplinary need and context is the overall expectation of the supervisor. This skill has been likened to the ability of the helicopter to hover above the scene while remaining close enough to zone in to any part of it as necessary - without getting so close that it loses its balance or gets sucked onto the ground, where it would become damaged and therefore useless.

Being self aware is a valuable attribute in many jobs. Using self awareness as a skill can be described as the professional use of self and thus enhances practice in a responsible, proactive way.

Insightful self awareness requires the ability to combine self awareness with insight into your own motivations and processes. This is not always an easy task. Many motivations and processes are "hidden" or "unknown". Skilled facilitation is required if what is hidden or unknown is to be confronted and acknowledged in a constructive manner.

The insightful self aware supervisor is more likely to facilitate effective Supervision than her colleague who may be operating from her own lack of awareness, personal motivations and subjective or reactive input.

## Using your senses through "total listening"

Listening is recognised as a key skill in any interpersonal engagement, however, "listening" in a professional context involves more than the ears. It requires the use of a range of senses.

To use "total listening" requires:

- Ears - to hear the words, the tone of voice, the pauses and the silence.

- Eyes - to notice the expressions, the body language and the "avoidances".
- Voice - to reflect back at times what has been said, to question for clarity, to reassure, to challenge and to give direction.
- Silence - to show respect, to give time for thought, to consider what is said, to move at the pace of the supervisee, to offer support and affirmation.
- "Gut" - to read between the lines, to use insight, and especially to connect to your own inner processes - awareness, reactions, blocks, biases and agenda.
- Body language, including eye contact - to convey messages of interest, understanding and attention.

There are two other aspects to listening that every supervisor would do well to master and they are:

- listening effectively when you are not interested in what is being said

and

- listening objectively when you are very interested in what is being said.

There may be times in Supervision with another when, for a variety of reasons, you find yourself uninterested in what is being said. This disinterest may be caused by a preoccupation with unfinished business prior to the Supervision meeting. It may be that you have heard the story before; it may be that you don't agree with the supervisee's account but you are hesitant or reluctant to say so. Whatever the reason, your disinterest is unfair and disrespectful to the supervisee. Over time, it can undermine and be potentially damaging to the Supervision.

It is the responsibility of the supervisor to prepare and be prepared for the Supervision they provide. This means finding ways to let go of, or put aside, other work for the duration of the meeting. It means doing your best to hear what is being said as the supervisee's experience and not as you perceive it to be. It means being honest with the supervisee, provided that the honesty is motivated by professional principles, by the functions of Supervision (accountability, support and learning) and by your responsibilities as supervisor.

Listening to someone when you are interested in what they are saying seems easy. However, it is all too easy to get drawn into the "story" of what you are hearing and to lose sight of your responsibility as a supervisor. This could lead to over-identification with the supervisee and a possible subjective response by you. This could be inappropriate and potentially detrimental to Supervision and to the supervisee in the long term. This is when your self awareness will help you to maintain objectivity, thereby "hovering" over what you hear in the context of your role and responsibilities as a supervisor.

Listening is never a passive activity and, having heard, you then share responsibility for the information you have been told and you need to make a conscious decision regarding the necessary course of action. This is one reason why you can never promise or even indicate that you will keep information to yourself in a professional context. The not unfamiliar comment, *"I don't want anyone to know this came from me but I think you should know that..."* has no place in professional communications. It contradicts the principles of accountable practice and contributes to closed, unhealthy and even abusive cultures.

It needs to be stressed that listening is not just the responsibility of the supervisor- the supervisee also shares responsibility for actively listening and for hearing what is said in Supervision.

# Feedback

Feedback is a necessary and significant part of professional practice; it is recognised as a vital component of Supervision. It requires understanding and skill on the part of the supervisor if it is to contribute effectively to the practice and process of Professional Supervision.

Feedback needs to be understood as a two-way process with responsibility for its effective implementation accepted by both the supervisee and the supervisor.
Too often feedback in Supervision has been perceived as the responsibility of the supervisor alone. Discussing the role of feedback together when entering into the Supervision partnership sets the expectation and responsibilities in place from the start.

Effective feedback should be an ongoing and seamless component of all Supervision, provided in a natural manner. Two-way feedback requires a culture of mutual respect and acceptance where both participants value what the other says and are open to learning from it.

It needs to be accurate and constructive and given in a way that will be of use to the receiver. It is necessary to know why the feedback is being given and what it intends to achieve. Frequently feedback is given in vague and general terms which do not contribute to improved or affirmed practice.

Think about these two comments:
> "That was a good report"
> "The report you wrote yesterday was well structured and the recommendations clearly highlighted important points"

Which would be more useful to hear?

The first comment may provide a "feel good" factor in the moment but do you really have any idea as to what made it a good report? If not, how can you recreate it knowingly the next time?

The second comment affirms specific aspects of the report which contribute not only to the writer feeling good but also to learning for future report writing.

Hawkins and Shohet (1994) suggest the following useful mnemonic as a means of remembering how to give good feedback

## CORBS

C Clear   Be clear in what you want to say and say it directly. This means you need to be aware of what you want to say and why you need to say it.

O Owned   You are giving your observation or experience of the other person, not a judgement.

R Regular   It is not useful to save up feedback and give it all in one go. Let it be an ongoing part of your direct communication, given as close to the event as possible.

B Balanced   Over time the feedback needs to be balanced. No matter how good a person's practice is, there is always room for improvement. No matter how poor a person's work might seem, they are doing something right.

S Specific   Feedback that is vague or general in content is frequently misunderstood and does not lead to learning. It is helpful to give an example or to identify the particular situation or behaviour.

Don't forget to ask for feedback if it is not forthcoming. Make sure it is clear, balanced and specific. Ask for examples if you are not sure what the person means. When someone gives you feedback it is important to listen to all of what is being said and not to respond or react defensively. Receiving feedback is valuable in helping you to hear and understand how another person finds you. It can be an opportunity to learn more about yourself (and maybe about the other person too).

# Questions and Questioning

The use of questions in Supervision demands an element of discipline on the part of the supervisor. Well-placed questions can add considerably to the benefits gained by the supervisee. Badly timed questions, asked for the wrong reasons, can not only block the flow of what is being said but can divert the content and also evoke feelings of insecurity and mistrust in the supervisee.

When asking a question during Supervision, the self aware supervisor will know why the question is being asked and its relevance to the supervisee at that time. If the question is to satisfy the supervisor's curiosity or to find out unnecessary information, then this is not an adequate reason for the question. On the other hand, if the question is to help relevant understanding of the topic being presented or is necessary to establish greater clarity and/or accountability for either the supervisor or the supervisee, then it must be asked.

The type of question used will influence the subsequent discussion. Consider the following types of questions and the possible responses - are they likely to open up the discussion or close it down? Which type of questions do you use most frequently and why?

Open Questions -  These invite comment and usually begin with words like who, what, why, where, when and how - the five Ws & how:
*What did you learn from that?*
*Why was the meeting changed?*
*Where were you when she spoke to you?*
*When did you become aware of the problem?*
*How did you manage to complete the work on time?*

Closed Questions - Usually invite a one-word (yes/no) answer, for example:
*Did you speak to her? Have you written the report? Are you alright?*

Probing Questions - Illicit further information -
*Tell me how that happened?
What did you see then?
How does that affect you?
What else was happening at the time?*

Circular and Reflexive Questions - Help to focus on wider thinking and open up new possibilities:
*What would you say if it happened again?
If the child's father was here now, what do you think he would say?
What will you be doing differently when things have improved?
What do you think your colleague would say about you in that situation?*

Reasoning Questions - Allow opportunity to explore reasons behind situations and often only require Why?
*Why did you decide to do it that way?
Why do you think it worked so well?*
It is important that Why questions are used to gain greater understanding and not as a form of interrogation

Prompting Questions- Helping the conversation along gently:
*And then what happened?
She said...?*

Clarifying
Questions -    Making sure that you are hearing what is meant
*Have I heard you right that you were confused about the directions you were given?*
*I just need to check that I understand you correctly, so you're saying that you think there was something else bothering the patient?*

Reflective
Questions -    Reflecting on the meaning of what you hear as well as the words:
*So you seem to have been very apprehensive about visiting the family alone?*

Leading
Questions -    Questions that lead the speaker to a specific answer can frequently indicate more about the questioner than it does about the speaker's opinion. On the whole they should be avoided:
*Did he do that?*
*I suppose you are annoyed about that?*

## Responding to Questions as a Supervisor

It is important that supervisors use their self-awareness in responding to questions posed by the supervisee. Questions will be asked for a variety of reasons. Some may need an immediate response but not all questions always require an immediate answer.

The newly recruited member of staff will undoubtedly require answers to information questions in order to carry out his responsibilities; however six months later it is reasonable to expect that the nature as well as the frequency of the questions will have altered.

It is not unusual for the new supervisor, when asked a specific question, to feel under pressure to know the answer or at the very least to assure the supervisee they will find out immediately. At times this is necessary - as in informing them of the policy or procedure relating to aspects of practice or providing specific background information to inform the direct work. There are other times when providing the immediate answer may not always be the most beneficial experience for the supervisee, as in the long term it may lead to abdication of responsibility or over-dependence on the supervisor, neither of which fit the objectives of Professional Supervision.

As well as experiencing pressure at times, the supervisor new to supervisory responsibility can be so relieved at being asked questions that she can answer that she rushes in with answers without thinking about whether it is the most appropriate response or not, thereby doing the supervisee a disservice as well as losing sight of self awareness and the importance of conscious intervention.

As in all aspects of Supervision it is necessary, when asking or responding to questions, to keep sight of whose needs are central to the process and practice - the needs of the supervisee to carry out their job, the needs of the organisation to ensure relevant effective care and service and ultimately the needs of the client/patient - not the needs of the supervisor as an individual.

Whatever the circumstances or nature of the questions posed by the supervisee, it is always necessary for the supervisor to respond in a responsible and self aware manner.

## "Games" in Supervision

A number of situations can develop in the supervisory partnership that need to be recognised in order to prevent them becoming blocks or "games" as described by Kadushin (1976). It is important that the supervisor

recognises what is happening at an early stage so that Supervision does not become diminished by unhealthy processes. Both supervisor and supervisee can be responsible for such "games" being introduced and used; it is however the responsibility of the supervisor to ensure that if such "games" enter into Supervision, that they are recognised and challenged in order to ensure that Supervision remains effective and focused on its objectives.
Below are some examples of the types of the situations, blocks, messages or "games" that all supervisors must be aware of if they are to avoid unhealthy processes in Supervision.

## *Supervisee Games*
- *We're short staffed*
- *I'm too busy for Supervision today*
- *I have too much to do*

This might be genuine occasionally but you need to be aware of the circumstances and discuss how Supervision is to be managed in the immediate circumstances. These reasons can also be used to avoid Supervision - if this is the case, it will sometimes require challenge by the supervisor and possibly a discussion to refocus on the purpose and function of Supervision.

- *Let me do my own thing*
- *Let me do it my way*
- *I don't need Supervision.*

This implies a direct avoidance of Supervision and can be displayed when the purpose and function of Supervision are not clear, understood or accepted. At times the worker who may have worked without any Supervision for years may feel that its introduction is a direct threat to their practice or a vote of no confidence in themselves. Alternatively it can happen when the supervisee lacks confidence in the person with supervisory responsibilities possibly believing that they themselves have more experience than the supervisor. They may in fact have more practice experience. It is also a fact that the supervisor has been given supervisory responsibilities by the organisation, this is usually in the context of their role and responsibilities within the workplace. Therefore, both partners have to find a way of working together for the benefit of the service users.

- *I have so much going on in my personal life, please don't bring up anything about my work*
- *"Treat me, don't beat me"*

In other words "I'm too full of my own personal problems for my work to be evaluated". The supervisee may well have significant things going on in their own life but that is not a reason for the supervisor to avoid addressing work issues as necessary. Nor is it a reason for the supervisor to facilitate personal disclosure by the supervisee. Messages like those above could be used as a "game" to prevent Supervision developing or for the supervisee to seek personal support - neither can be allowed.

- *I will tell you this but you cannot say I told you*
- *I need you to keep this confidential*

As a supervisor you do not have the right to agree to such requests. These comments bring up issues around limits, boundaries, confidentiality and possible collusive relationships which must be addressed between supervisor and supervisee. Professional relationships and the accountability attached to them need attention and understanding to be effective.

- *I have done a thesis on Supervision*
- *In my previous job the Supervision was always excellent*
- *I have years of Supervision experience*

This can be genuine and of use if it is used as a backdrop to understanding the supervisee's previous experience and expectations of Supervision. It could, on the other hand, at times be used as a block to entering into the supervisory process with a new supervisor. Recounting superior knowledge or experience can give the message, "I know better than you" or "I will be comparing" and thus attempt to disempower the supervisor. As a supervisor it is good to remember that knowledge of Supervision is different to the skill of supervising!

- *You don't work with me*
- *You are the manager, you don't really know what it's like to work on the floor*
- *You're too removed from the work to understand what I'm going through*
- *What do you know, you sit in your office*

These messages can be used in an attempt to block Supervision or to disempower the supervisor. It is not necessary for the supervisor to be totally familiar with every aspect of the supervisee's daily practice in order to be effective. It is the responsibility of the supervisee to come to Supervision prepared and capable of presenting their points clearly for discussion (although for some this can take time to develop and then becomes part of Supervision itself)

- *You're wonderful...*

This could be used to sidetrack or distract from the agenda. Also, it is difficult to be critical while being flattered.

Remember however that two-way feedback is an integral component of all effective Supervision. Positive feedback from the supervisee is to be welcomed (as is the not so positive) provided it is relevant, specific and not overdone.

It is not only supervisees who play "games" in Supervision; Supervisors can enter into "game" playing too.

## Supervisor Games

- *I know you've got difficulties but wait until I tell you about mine!*

Supervision is for the supervisee and not the place for the supervisor to discuss his/her problems. Neither is Supervision about providing support for the supervisor.

- *I'm around a lot longer than you (so I know better)*

Supervisors can sometimes mean to help by using such messages but in effect this type of message usually disempowers the supervisee and acts as a block to their development and confidence as well as coming across as a "put down" or defensiveness on the part of the supervisor.

- *You have no idea how busy I am today*
- *I have a really important meeting in an hour*

This is allowing outside factors to distract from the Supervision process and frequently gives the supervisee the message that the needs of the supervisor are more important than those of the supervisee. It can also be a subtle (or at times not so subtle) way of putting pressure on the supervisee to hurry up. Expecting the supervisee to enter into Supervision in such circumstances is not only unfair but can also be perceived as disrespectful.

- *I was only trying to help*

This comes across as defensive against criticism from the supervisee.

> *"Games lead to avoidance of responsibility and poor decision making. Supervisors have to unmask the game and refuse to play."*
> (Moore, 1997)

## Intervention Approaches

It is important that all supervisors have a range of interventions to draw from in Supervision to ensure its effective use. Heron (1975) identified six categories of intervention used in any facilitating process. Knowing what they are helps the supervisor to identify which ones they are most comfortable with and which ones may require further development. Most people have a natural tendency towards some of these identified approaches and regularly use them, while subconsciously avoiding others. None of the identified intervention approaches are more or less useful than the others. Being aware of them and knowing when to use different ones and in what circumstances adds greatly to the skill of the supervisor and thereby to the overall effectiveness of Supervision.

In reading the following, identify the intervention approaches with which you are most comfortable or familiar. Consider circumstances in which a different approach may be worth trying, particularly if you find yourself "stuck" in the supervisory process with another. It is also worth reflecting on why you veer towards some approaches rather than others.

The following are the intervention approaches as identified by Heron (1975)

- Prescriptive    Giving advice, being direct in what you say
  e.g. "You need to go and talk to Johnny about that"
- Informative    Instructing or informing the supervisee
  e.g. "The policy is…" or "This is how we deal with that request"
- Confrontative   Giving direct feedback, being challenging
  e.g. "I notice that you always start by mentioning Tommy"
- Cathartic    Giving an opportunity to release tension
  e.g. "What would you really like to say?"
- Catalytic    Encouraging the supervisee to reflect and consider their options, "What can you do about that?", "What other options are there?"
- Supportive    Affirming or validating the supervisee's ideas or actions
  e.g. "That is very clear" or "It seems as if you followed through on the decision confidently"

> "These six types of intervention are only of any real value if they are rooted in care and concern for the client or supervisee."
> (Hawkins and Shohet 1994)

One of the many tasks of the supervisor is to evoke curiosity in the supervisee to contribute to their ongoing development and motivation. This can be achieved through reflection, genuine interest and the sharing of constructive feedback delivered in an atmosphere of respect and safety.

The supervisor's ability to actively Listen, to Affirm positive aspects of practice and to appropriately Challenge are some of the skills identified by supervisees as being most beneficial to them in Supervision.

# *Supervising the Student*

Practice Placements form an integral part of qualifying courses for many professionals. As far back as 1917, when the Edinburgh University Social Studies course was started, it was decided that students would spend approximately one half of their training in practice placements. This tradition continues today to varying degrees. Social Work, Social Care, Psychology, Nursing, Occupational Therapy, Speech and Language Therapy, Teaching and the Gardaí, are among disciplines that provide a practice element to qualifying courses for their students.

The placement requires students to consider the "fit" between theory and practice in order to develop competence in "applying" theory and skills. It provides the opportunity to develop insightful awareness in their chosen career path. Placements can also provide an opportunity to establish the student's suitability for the work and to clarify their preferred area of practice. The primary purpose of any placement experience for the student is to be afforded the opportunity to "test out" their knowledge and skills within the safety of a well structured and supervised work setting. The direction and guidance of an experienced, competent professional facilitates the training of the student throughout.

The first introduction for the majority of professionals to Supervision is during their student days as part of the practice placement component of their qualifying courses. Early experiences can have a profound and lasting impact on how professionals view and later use Supervision.

Some students find their introduction to Supervision in the workplace a positive and worthwhile engagement. It allows them time and structure to reflect on their experiences and enables them to begin to make sense of what is happening around them in the context of the more formal and theoretical learning of the college environment. In other words, they are facilitated in a structured and supportive manner to connect theory to practice. They then begin the process of integrating their learning into practice so that it becomes part of the way they work in a conscious manner.

Other students however find Supervision to be a time of tension. It offers them little more than a brief opportunity to receive direction or correction on their efforts. Little time, if any, is given to discussion on their working experiences, let alone time for consideration of any ideas of their own. Neither are they facilitated to explore the fit between their theoretical knowledge and their experience of practice. In such circumstances, it is understandable that students begin to see Supervision as something to be avoided or just "got through" in order to fulfil the placement requirements as set down by the college.

To be fair to those who supervise students, they often do so without any consideration made to an already over stretched and frequently pressurised workload and often with the minimum, if any, input or training as to what is required of the supervisor of a student on placement. The situation is not as bleak as this for some disciplines. The advent of some basic input from a growing number of colleges for those undertaking the Supervision of students is improving the situation; however, it is far from comprehensive. Such input would benefit from further structured development. This would ensure that the student is not at the mercy of individual supervisor's interpretation of Supervision (and indeed placement expectations). Being exposed to an ad hoc experience of Supervision can colour the student's attitude for years to come.

The reservations and resistance that can at times be experienced with some individuals long after qualifying, can often be traced back to the early Supervision they received (or did not receive) as students. The attitude of the service or organisation to Supervision is also a significant factor in the developing attitude of the student and can have far-reaching effects in later years. It is worth remembering that attitudes are caught - not taught. A service that only goes through the motions of providing Supervision or says one thing in its policy but whose actual practice is different, is providing contradictory messages to the student who is in the process of forming their understanding of professionalism.

As the numbers being admitted to many qualifying courses increase in the current climate of greater demand for workers in certain professions and with the focus in third level colleges, as in other areas, on increased return, it is reasonable that the requirement for greater numbers of placements is also increasing. In such circumstances it is more than ever imperative that the workplace has clear policies and structures in place for student placements in general and for the effective professional Supervision of each student in particular. The collaboration between the colleges and workplaces providing placements is vital if the needs of the students are to be effectively met.

Students, as well as qualified workers, are entitled to Supervision that is professional in its practice and process. To ensure this, it is important that any organisation or department, which offers placement experiences to students of third level qualifying courses, does so in an informed and responsible manner in keeping with professional boundaries and educational requirements.

Student Supervision should allow structured regular periods of time where the student and the supervisor can reflect on the student's work experience and ensure that learning takes place.

Any discussion of the student's work needs to take into account not only what the student is engaged in but must also focus on *how* the work is carried out. This introduces the student to the importance of process as well as content - an important component in ongoing and lifelong development which is mirrored in the *Dual Focus Approach* within Supervision.

Most colleges will have particular requirements regarding student placements - for example, the overall objectives of the placement, the assessment criteria and the frequency and duration of Supervision.

The following provides guidelines for the Supervision meeting between student and supervisor

*Figure 4*

### Guidelines for Supervising the Student

**Planned Time:**
- Prearranged meetings
- Preferably weekly - one-hour duration
- Uninterrupted
- Agenda - both supervisor and student should have input to the agenda

## *Use the time to:*
- Reflect on the week - positive experiences as well as areas of difficulty
- Discuss ideas about what has happened - the student's ideas as well as the supervisor's and consider what may have contributed to such events
- Ensure the standard of practice - the supervisor is responsible and accountable insofar as possible for the student's practice
- Give and seek specific feedback
- Consider the impact of the work on the student - for example: frustrating, exciting, overwhelming, sadness, enthusiastic, upsetting
- Allow for the connection of theory to the practice being experienced in the workplace - for example, get the student to focus on why certain things may be happening and how this fits in with particular theories they have studied
- Identify any gaps which may emerge in the student's knowledge base relevant to the work setting and direct to source or inform as necessary
- Discuss written reports (if any) - consider the style as well as the content
- Plan the aims for the coming week and identify tasks to achieve them
- Arrange the date and time of the next Supervision meeting
- Record the meeting with the student and both sign it

Throughout Supervision, remember, as the supervisor, to give regular, specific and balanced feedback, and to be supportive and honest.

- if there are difficulties or problems - say so
- if things are going well - tell the student.

Used in this way the student is effectively introduced to the practice and process of professional Supervision in a manner likely to foster their responsible participation from the outset of their careers.
Remember, as supervisor you must

    *- Encourage*

    *- Support*

    *- Direct and Guide*

    *- Challenge and*

    *- Affirm*

# Case Studies

The following case studies are a composite of Supervision experiences and provide examples of the reality of Professional Supervision.

### Case Study 1 - Lillian

*Lillian completed a National Diploma in Applied Social Studies in Social Care fifteen months ago. She spent six months working in a community based after-school project for young children and eight weeks ago began work in a residential childcare centre in a unit providing care to young people aged 10-15.*

*Two of these young people often use explicit sexualised language, which they can direct at staff in a personal way. She had heard from other staff, who were all there longer than her, that one of the boys, Tommy, could be very threatening towards staff. Although Lillian has never seen any of this behaviour herself she is wary of Tommy and seems to avoid getting into any direct confrontations with him. Past experience of this shows that, if not dealt with, this situation can provide Tommy with the opportunity of taking control - not a situation that is safe for him.*

*Lillian comes to Supervision and seems tense although she says that she is getting on "o.k." and that everything is 'fine'. When asked about what specifically is 'fine', her eye contact breaks completely and she appears more uneasy than before. The supervisor, who says that it can be difficult at times in the early days, acknowledges this sensitively. She adds that she has noticed that Lillian seems to be spending less time with Tommy than with the other children and asks her if there is something on her mind, at which point she becomes more uneasy and begins to explain that she is afraid of being hit by Tommy. This is explored further and it becomes clear that Lillian has not said this to anyone for fear that the staff will think that she can't cope or that there is something wrong with her.*

*A number of factors were considered in the next half hour and it emerged that her fear and anxiety had paralysed her from using her knowledge of child development, which was extensive, and her skills of communication where Tommy was concerned. It emerged that she had observed and discovered quite a lot about Tommy in 8 weeks, including the fact that he followed Chelsea Football Club because his older brother did. She knew that he had a real interest in history and enjoyed stories based on life long ago rather than science fiction or 'made up stories' as he called them. He loved jokes and was always looking for new ones. She had also observed that Tommy could be particularly demanding of certain staff and that he responded well to individual attention.*

*At this point Lillian had relaxed and was talking freely and positively about Tommy. She had identified aspects of Tommy that she found interesting and potentially useful for relating to him in the future. With prompting, she then made suggestions about how she might respond the next time Tommy became threatening towards her and considered her options. She was now seeing Tommy in a broader context and she was not as paralysed by one aspect of Tommy's behaviour. Lillian agreed to talk to other members of the team about the situation and was assured that finding aspects of the work difficult was not unusual nor did what was happening mean she couldn't cope. However, it did indicate that she needed to be more open about how the work was affecting her so that she could consider how to deal with it. To finish this Supervision meeting, the main points discussed and the decisions made as a result were recorded by Lillian and the Supervisor together. Lillian, at a later meeting said the record had given her something tangible to consider and also a way of reminding herself of the changes that had occurred as a result.*

*Six months and many Supervision sessions later, Lillian and the supervisor reviewed this earlier meeting and considered the factors that had contributed to its effectiveness.*

The following points emerged from the review and highlight many significant factors.

1. Supervision was prearranged for all staff - everyone in the service attended regular Supervision and not just those new to the job. This Lillian found, helped her to be open to, and more accepting of, the process.
2. The supervisor had knowledge of the situation, the child and of Lillian.
3. 'Fine' was not just accepted - it was explored.
4. Permission was given for it to be "o.k." that there might be a problem - this provided safety.
5. The tension and anxiety displayed by Lillian were acknowledged by the supervisor.
6. Lillian's initial fear of Tommy was considered and given time so that the other fear of 'not coping' emerged.
7. Lillian regained interest and confidence through identifying positive aspects of Tommy.
8. She reflected on some theoretical aspects of child development, particularly in relation to separation and loss, which were significant in relation to Tommy.
9. She considered realistic options for relating to Tommy.
10. She agreed to discuss it with team members, thereby looking for constructive support and further feedback.
11. Lillian left with a plan - this she found empowered her and gave her a tangible reference on which she later reflected.

## Case study 2 - **Jim**

*Jim is a Principal Social Worker in a Health Board community care team. He manages a staff of fifteen, from basic grade to team leader grade. Over the years Jim has always worked to maintain staff morale and encourage development.*

*The service is currently undergoing significant change to meet current demands. The strict enforcement of employment ceilings and financial constraints are placing enormous strains on frontline managers. They are under pressure from a number of competing forces, namely from the staff to provide more resources and better working conditions, from the public to meet ever-higher expectations and from their line managers to work within existing resources and produce better outcomes.*

*With one vacancy on the team for the last four months, some key staff have left recently, one to relocate, another to a better position with a private service provider and one person is on long term sick leave due to stress.*

*His line manager has informed Jim that a number of immediate cost savings have been identified across all services. The four vacant posts are not being filled in the foreseeable future and Jim is expected to ensure that the travel expenses of his department are cut back until a review takes place at the end of the year. He is aware that some staff are very resistant to any change. He has to achieve some sort of balance between meeting the demands of the Health Board and still facilitating the staff in providing a tenable service to the clients.*

*In this context Jim comes to Supervision feeling very disillusioned and uncertain about his abilities to continue to manage effectively.*

*How do you think the supervisor might fulfil his role and responsibilities to Jim?*

*He could just empathise with Jim and only facilitate a venting about the vagaries of service and staff. However if the functions of Supervision are adhered to, then the focus will also be on allowing Jim to explore how he can manage the immediate needs of the department while identifying realistic goals for himself and for the team.*

*Keeping the balance between accountability, support and learning in mind, the supervisor uses a catalytic intervention to facilitate Jim to reflect on his practice and on his current difficulties. He uses open and circular questioning to elicit what has worked well for Jim in the past and to explore what he feels may be improved in the immediate as well as the long term. The subsequent discussion allows the opportunity to validate judgement calls and acknowledge positive outcomes.*

*Through reflection, Jim identifies what has succeeded in the past and how he might replicate some of that again, - particularly in relation to managing staff, as this was his major concern in the light of ever increasing pressures on them and him. This provides more objectivity to the current situation and begins to regenerate energy for the task ahead, notwithstanding the significant difficulties which are acknowledged by both Jim and his supervisor.*

*Jim is informed by his supervisor of some of the long term plans and objectives for the department with the ongoing changes to be implemented over the coming months. This challenges him positively and constructively to consider the wider picture and how his work could develop. On reflection, Jim identifies that this was something that was bothering him but he had not necessarily thought it through prior to Supervision as he had concentrated his concerns on the staff.*

*Throughout Supervision Jim was challenged to step outside the immediate issues and to consider how he and the team fit into the larger picture. He feels more assured and has agreed a plan of action to review some specific aspects of practice and options with the team. Among other things, this may include sharing case loads based on geographical locations. In summarising the Supervision, Jim used it to focus on his abilities in the context of his role and responsibilities in the overall and ongoing development and delivery of services.*

These are two very different examples of Supervision which highlight some of the factors which contribute to its effective and varied uses. No two Supervision meetings are ever the same, just as no two people are the same. Different interventions, styles and approaches are required, depending, not only on the person and their stage of professional development but also on the immediate situations presented. The experienced supervisor will have the ability to adapt to such differences while always maintaining the principles of Professional Supervision.

# *Beginnings and Endings*

A significant amount of attention is usually paid to the beginning of the supervisory partnership. The importance of introducing Supervision and the initial engagement between supervisee and supervisor; the role of contracting and how to go about drawing up and recording the contract; the need to establish a connection between the supervisor and supervisee and the "tuning in time", are all areas which get considerable thought and time at the beginning of the supervisory engagement.

Indeed this is reflected at organisational level when Supervision is first introduced to the service or discipline. Time is invested in considering not only the policy but also the structures and procedures to facilitate the most productive use of the resource of Supervision. Consideration is given to who will have responsibility for supervising whom and hopefully to how the service will monitor and evaluate this new practice and process. All of these things are vital and need attention if Supervision is to be effective. Setting the context, identifying responsibilities and establishing contact, all contribute to the beginnings of Supervision.

## Starting Supervision

The following provides guidelines on areas for inclusion in a first meeting between a supervisor and supervisee. As with all guidelines they should not be considered in isolation but should be viewed in the context of agency, organisation and discipline requirements and discussed in relation to the service policy.

*Figure 5*

---

**Guidelines for an introductory Supervision meeting between a Supervisor and new Supervisee**

**Tune in to each other regarding Supervision**
- Share overall Supervision experiences to date
- Identify similarities and differences

**Consider why Supervision is required as an integral part of professional practice**
- in general
- in this service/job

**Identify what is meant by Supervision** - be specific

**Outline and discuss how Supervision will be provided and used.** This can be done in the context of reviewing the Supervision Policy or through a general discussion.
The following points need to be clarified:

- Frequency of meetings
- Boundaries/Confidentiality
- Agenda
- Difficulties
- Ongoing Review of Supervision

- Duration of meetings
- Responsibilities of each
- Recording
- Specific needs or requirements

**Contract/Agreement**

**Review the meeting** - get and give feedback

**Record** the main points together and both sign

**Arrange date for the next meeting**

# Ending Supervision

Just as importantly as the beginning is how Supervision ends. Frequently though, not as much attention gets paid to the ending of Supervision. The ending of Supervision demands thought, planning, reflection and at times, sensitivity. There are usually two reasons that Supervision between the two participants comes to an end. Either, when someone leaves the service or when someone moves within the service and thereby changes supervisor.

There are significant benefits to working towards bringing Supervision to an effective end.
- Firstly, the supervisee gets the opportunity to recognise in a structured way the contributions they have made to the service and at the same time identifies their own growth and development.
- Secondly, the supervisor gains valuable feedback on themselves as a supervisor. This provides useful material for the supervisor who constructively and proactively attends to their own ongoing development.
- Thirdly are the benefits to the organisation as a whole. Feedback, sought in a genuine and realistic manner, has the potential to contribute insight to the workings of the organisation. If the person is leaving the service, the final Supervision meeting can act as an exit interview. This can provide valuable feedback to the service for its future development if the Supervision meeting is conducted in a structured manner with an identified and effective feedback loop at organisational level.

Entering into Supervision with another, whether as supervisor or as supervisee requires commitment, energy, honesty, responsibility and a certain investment of oneself. Planning is necessary to bring such a process to an effective close. A certain element of letting go is required. This is usually achieved by looking back, by acknowledging the present and by looking forward to the ongoing development and work of the supervisee. It includes overall feedback by both participants on the experience of

Supervision as well as on changes which may have occurred or may be useful for the future.

Used in this way, the final Supervision meeting includes significant reflection and balanced feedback between both participants. As such, the final meeting has the potential for improved insight and self awareness for each person.

Remembering that Supervision is a process, it is equally important to recognise that bringing Supervision to a satisfactory conclusion is also a process. In reality, and allowing for time constraints, one or two meetings usually form the core of this closing process.

There are times when the Supervision partnership will come to an end, not because either person is leaving the service, but for other reasons. It may be due to internal transfer or a change in role of one or the other or it may be the policy of the organisation to ensure that people periodically receive different Supervision experiences through planned changes. If this is the case, it may be useful to consider the transfer arrangements as it is important that a level of continuity is built in, particularly for the supervisee. (See appendix 3 for a sample of a Transfer Sheet)

Below are some general guidelines on the areas to be considered in final Supervision meetings between the participants. Again, they are offered as guidelines only and should not be seen as a complete agenda in themselves. The requirements will differ depending on whether the participants are leaving the service or changing supervisory partners while remaining in the service.

*Figure 6*

Page 1 of 2

## Guidelines for Concluding the Supervision partnership between the Supervisee and Supervisor when either one is changing role or leaving the service

Based on advance notice and preparation by both people, final Supervision meeting/s will benefit from attention to a number of factors in relation to two main areas:
1. The overall experience of the work
2. The experience of Supervision

**Tune in** to each other and acknowledge what it is like meeting in this context for the last time/s.

**Unfinished aspects**
Ensure that ongoing work has been handed over appropriately to identified colleagues.
Consider current work and any aspects which may be unfinished or left hanging for the supervisee. Explore ways of completing and letting go. Anything that may need to be addressed or identified with others prior to leaving?

**Reflection**
Reflect on the overall experience of working in the service including the experience of Supervision.
Consider difficulties experienced throughout and factors which helped or hindered.
Explore and identify the high points and what made them high points. Consider any changes or differences the supervisee has noticed in themselves since working together.
Any regrets? If so, what are they? and why do they exist?

"Guidelines for Concluding" continued

**Feedback**
Offer specific feedback on aspects of particular strength and areas of development noticed in the supervisee and in their practice.
Seek feedback on the supervisee's experience of working in the service and in Supervision, what worked and what blocked the experiences.
Ask for suggestions on how the overall experiences could have been improved or more useful.
Identify and discuss areas requiring further development in the supervisee.
Acknowledge the input and effort of the supervisee overall and particularly in Supervision.

**Moving on**
What will the supervisee take with them to the new workplace or role from the experiences gained?
What do they hope to leave behind?
What will they say to a new supervisor about what they like, want or need from Supervision? What do they not want?
Affirm the positive developments in the supervisee and locate them in the new role and responsibilities of the supervisee, if appropriate.

**Remember as supervisor you also need to consider how you "let go" of your work with supervisees, particularly at times of high staff turnover. Use your own Supervision for this.**

# *"What if....?"*

In the training of supervisors and supervisees it is usual to encounter a range of what if...? questions. This section considers a small selection of frequently posed what ifs......and, though not attempting to suggest that there is only one answer or that there is a simple answer, provides comment on each which may trigger insight or ideas to the reader in dealing with them.

- ***What if we are finished with the agenda in 30 minutes, should we end the meeting then?***
  If an hour has been allocated for Supervision then it is reasonable to expect that the full time will be used effectively. Cutting down on the time given to Supervision can imply a lack of clarity or understanding regarding its purpose and functions. The challenge to some supervisors and supervisees, if this occurs, is to refocus on the wider uses of Supervision. Be careful that the above question is not driven by a lack of commitment to the process as well as the practice of Supervision by either participant.

  People work approximately between 132 and 156 hours per month and having one hour in this time to reflect on their role, responsibilities and practice as well as considering their skills and areas for ongoing development is not an excessive amount of time and needs to be used effectively.

- **What if the supervisee regularly has no agenda?**
  Maybe the supervisee is unsure of what to bring to Supervision or it may be that in past experiences of Supervision the supervisor held full responsibility for the agenda.

  In such situations, it may be necessary to offer some support and guidance. It can be useful to refocus on the purpose and function of Supervision within the service. A discussion on how both participants are experiencing Supervision is useful in such circumstances. Initially it may be necessary for the supervisor to ask the supervisee to bring, to the next meeting, specific examples of practice which he is finding worthwhile or those which are particularly demanding. This provides a focus for discussion and the potential for increased self awareness through reflection. It can also widen the supervisee's understanding and use of Supervision.
  If however, the supervisee continues to present unprepared for Supervision or if the supervisor has reason to believe that she is only going through the motions of participating in the process then the supervisor needs to consider different approaches. This may involve a more direct or confrontative engagement with clear expectations identified.

- **What do I do when the supervisee says everything is "Fine" and has nothing more to add?**
  Maybe things are fine for the supervisee. In which case it is necessary for the supervisor to accept this and not to attempt to search for difficulties where none may exist. In such circumstances it can be beneficial for the supervisee to be given the opportunity to identify, with examples, what is going well and to consider what may be contributing to this, with particular attention to what they themselves are doing to help the situation. The awareness thus gained could then be connected to other examples of practice with future benefit. It is vital that supervisors

use opportunities to "hold" and value positive experiences and practices. This is particularly necessary in some organisations where so much attention is regularly focused on what is not going well.

It must be remembered that Supervision is not only about problems. It has a range of uses and these may need to be explored with the supervisee who regularly presents with "Fine" and nothing more.

If however the supervisor has reason to think that everything is not fine or that the supervisee is blocking their engagement in Supervision through deflection, then the supervisor has a responsibility to check this out or confront it.

- *How do I manage to finish on time without appearing rude if the supervisee still wants to discuss something?*
Learning how to manage time is a requirement of practitioners in all areas of their work. Managing time in Supervision requires a clear focus by both participants. Agreement from the outset on the purpose and function of Supervision, identifying the time available and clarity surrounding the agenda with priorities stated at the start of each meeting all contribute to the time being well structured.

The supervisor has responsibility to ensure that the time is used effectively, this means knowing when and how to "move on". While it is important not to drag out the discussion just to fill the time it is equally important not to jump from point to point in order to touch on everything.

If the agenda is prioritised then the supervisor is more likely to keep track of the time with the remaining items in mind. Stating this can be beneficial in encouraging the supervisee to share responsibility for bringing Supervision to a close in the allocated time. For example "I notice that we have fifteen minutes left and we still have two items on the agenda, so what do we need to do now to ensure that we finish on time?"

- *If we don't get on, can we change supervisor/supervisee?*
There is an expectation in professional practice that people find ways of working together whether they "get on" or not. Supervision is part of professional practice and requires that the participants in the process work together towards effective engagement. This can be difficult for some who may be hesitant to acknowledge their unease for a variety of reasons and in such circumstances it is possible that Supervision is experienced as just going through the motions rather than a responsible engagement.

Changing partner is not necessarily the answer, however tempting. Those who use the services provided by the social worker, the nurse, the psychologist or the social care worker do not always have a choice regarding who they see or who will work with them. They are expected, often at times of vulnerability or need in their lives, to "get on with" the professional and find a way to work together.

Both supervisor and supervisee have a responsibility to ensure honest and effective communication as professionals. Finding a way to work together for the benefit of those who use the services is a challenge which can add greatly to the development of professional practice.

As you read this and further engage in the process of Supervision your own "what ifs...?" will emerge. Hopefully this book may have given you some ideas or insights to what lies behind some of the *what ifs...?* and maybe even sparked your thoughts about possible ways of dealing with them for yourself.

Professional Supervision has, in recent times, become expected and accepted as part of professional practice in many organisations. Nonetheless, the need for further understanding, regarding its use and benefits, is evident in the variety of ways in which it is carried out in different agencies. To ensure that Professional Supervision is used effectively as a resource for all (clients, staff and service) further understanding and skills are necessary. Professional Supervision needs to be seen, not as an individual activity, taking place in isolation but rather as a process in the context of an overall framework for professional practice.

When used properly, Professional Supervision is an invaluable resource which contributes to the ongoing development of responsible and responsive services. It can provide a structure for the individual, the team and the organisation to be purposefully supported and challenged and in the process of reflection to ensure ongoing learning for the ultimate benefit of those who use the services.

APPENDIX 1.

## *Professional Supervision Contract*

To implement the Professional Supervision Policy and Procedures of _____ *(service name)* the following details have been agreed between

_____ Supervisee

_____ Supervisor

Location of meetings _____

Frequency of supervision_____ Duration_____

Review arrangements and date/s _____

_____

_____

_____

Any other specific requirements/needs_____

_____

_____

_____

Signed _____ Date_____

Signed _____ Date_____

APPENDIX 2.

# *Professional Supervision Recording Sheet*

Supervision - One-to-one _____ Group _____ Team _____

Service/Department _____

Supervisee _____ Position _____

Supervisor _____ Position _____

Date _____ Time. _____

Agenda

| Supervisee | Supervisor |
|---|---|
|  |  |
|  |  |
|  |  |
|  |  |
|  |  |

Follow on items from last Supervision (if any) _____

_____

_____

_____

APPENDIX 2.                                              Page 2 of 2

Summary of discussion _____
_____
_____
_____
_____
_____
_____
_____
_____
_____
_____

| Decisions made | Responsibility of | Date |
|---|---|---|
|  |  |  |
|  |  |  |
|  |  |  |

Next Supervision meeting  _____

Signed
Supervisee_____ Date _____
Supervisor_____ Date _____

APPENDIX 3.  Page 1 of 2.

## *Supervision Transfer Form*

When changing supervisor within the same service this form is to be completed between the supervisor (to date) and the supervisee together on conclusion of their supervisory partnership. This completed form can then inform the agenda at the first meeting between the staff member and the new supervisor. Following this the form is kept with the Supervision records.

Supervisee_____ Supervisor_____

Service/Department_____

Date of first Supervision _____ Date of Final Supervision_____

1. Summary of main areas covered in Supervision (identify any particular issues, difficulties, skills and strengths and how these were addressed)

_____
_____
_____
_____
_____
_____
_____
_____
_____
_____
_____

APPENDIX 3.                                          Page 2 of 2.

2. Current areas being considered

_____
_____
_____
_____
_____
_____
_____

3. Points for ongoing development/ attention in the new supervisory partnership

_____
_____
_____
_____
_____
_____
_____
_____

Signed: Staff member _____ Date_____

Supervisor (to date) _____ Date_____

The above has been discussed between the new partners

Signed: Staff member_____ Date_____

Supervisor (new)_____ Date_____

# Reference and Bibliography

| | |
|---|---|
| An Bord Altranais (2000) | **Review of Scope of Practice for Nursing and Midwifery - Final Report** <br> An Bord Altranais : Dublin |
| Biestek (1961) | **The Casework Relationship** <br> Routledge: London |
| Braten (1983) | Cited in Hawkins and Shohet (1994) **Supervision in the Helping Professions** <br> Open University Press: Milton Keynes |
| Brown and Bourne (1996) | **The Social Work Supervisor** <br> Open University Press: Buckingham |
| Butterworth & Faugier (1992) | **Clinical Supervision and Mentorship in Nursing** <br> Chapman and Hall: London |
| Corcoran (1999) | **An Exploration of circular and reflexive questions in Residential Child Care Practice Supervision** <br> Dissertation - Masters in Family Therapy: Unpublished |
| Department of Health and Children (1999) | **Children First: National Guidelines for the Protection and Welfare of Children.** <br> Government Publications: Dublin |
| Department of Health and Children (2001) | **National Health Strategy; Quality and Fairness -** <br> A Health System for you. <br> Government Publications: Dublin |

| | |
|---|---|
| Department of Health and Children (2002) | **Action Plan for People Management in the Health Services**<br>Health Service Employers Agency: Dublin |
| Department of Health and Children (2001) | **National Standards for Children's Residential Centres.**<br>Government Publications: Dublin |
| Devonshire (1997) | **Continuing Professional Development**<br>Clinical Psychology Forum 99 |
| Donohoe (1996) | **Report of the Inquiry into the Operation of Madonna House.**<br>Department of Health: Dublin |
| Eardly (2002) | **Bullying and Stress in the Workplace**<br>First Law Limited: Dublin |
| Easterby - Smith et al (1991) | **Management Research: An Introduction**<br>Sage Publications: London |
| Ford and Jones (1987) | **Student Supervision**<br>Macmillan Press: London |
| Fulham (1997) | **Staff Retention problems in Community Care Social Work: the causes and the cure** |
| Graham (1994) | "The Roles of the Residential Care Worker" **in The Journal of the European Association of Training Centres For Socio-Educational Care Work:** Italy |
| Goldson (1995) | **A Sense of Security, Circular for the Induction and Training of Staff in Secure Accommodation**<br>National Children's Bureau: London |

| | |
|---|---|
| Handy (1985) | **Understanding Organisations**<br>Penguin Business: London |
| Hawkins and Shohet (1989 & 1994) | **Supervision in the Helping Professions**<br>Open University Press: Milton Keynes |
| Heron (1975)<br>University of Surrey | **Six Category Intervention Analysis.** |
| Kadushin (1976) | **Supervision in Social Work,**<br>Columbia University Press: New York |
| Kahan et al (1986) | **Staff, Finding Them, Choosing Them, Keeping Them**<br>Social Care Association: UK |
| Knapman and Morrison (2001) | **Making the Most of Supervision in Health and Social Care,** Pavilion: Brighton |
| Laming (2003) | **Victoria Climbié Inquiry**<br>H.M.S.O., London |
| Lewis and Batey (1982) | Clarifying autonomy and accountability in nursing service: Part 2 **Journal of Nursing Administration.** October 10-15. |
| McGuinness (1993) | **The Kilkenny Incest Investigation Report**<br>Government Publications Office: Dublin |
| Marsh and Triseliotis (1996) | **Ready to Practice?**<br>Avebury Press: U.K. |

Moore (1997) — Child Protection - Supervision in Social Service Departments in Edited by Pritchard; **Good Practice in Supervision** Jessica Kingsley Publishers:London

Morrison (1995)& (2002) — **Staff Supervision in Social Care** Pavilion Publishing: U.K.

National Health Strategy (2000) — **National Children's Strategy** Government Publications: Dublin

North Western Health Board (1998) — **Report of Inquiry into the West of Ireland Farmer Case** North Western Health Board, Manorhamilton

Office for Health Management (2003) — **Personal Development Planning,** Office for Health Management: Dublin

ONeill (2000) — **Professional Supervision in Social Care** Resident Managers Association

O Neill (2002) — The Practice of Professional Supervision in Residential Child Care **European Journal of Social Education** FESET

Ouchi and Johnson (1978) — Cited in Hawkins and Shohet (1994) **Supervision in the Helping Professions** Open University Press: U.K

Pedler et al (1997) — **The Learning Company.** McGraw-Hill: London

Power (1997) — **A Review of the Supervisory Practices of Clinical Psychologists in an Irish Health Authority Region:** Unpublished

Proctor (1986)    A Co-operative exercise in Accountability, in Marken and Payne eds. **Enabling and Ensuring:** National Youth Bureau and Council for Education and Training in Youth and Community Work: Leicester

Richards and Payne    **Staff Supervision in Child Protection Work**
(1990)    National Institute for Social Work: London

Sinclair and Gibbs (1998)    **Children's Homes - A Study in Diversity**
Wiley: England

Skinner (1992)    **Another Kind of Home;**
**A Review of Residential Care**
H.M.S.O. Edinburgh

Wiener (1997)    Supervision in Residential/Day Care Settings in Pritchard ed.
**Good Practice in Supervision**
Jessica Kingsley Publishers: London